Tea with Mister George

AND OTHER ADVENTURES IN MONTREAL

To Doug
Hope this
brings you
to visit here
(again)
Barry Lazar

Barry Lazar

Book design and cover design: Rita Bauer
Printed and bound in Canada by Marc Veilleux Imprimeur Inc.

Canadian cataloguing in publication data

Lazar, Barry, 1949 -
    Tea with Mr. George

ISBN 0-9683004-0-5

1. Montréal (Québec) - Description
2. Montréal (Québec) - Sanity
I. Title

Dépôt légal, Bibliothèque nationale du Québec and the
National Library of Canada.

Distributed by:
Barry Lazar
blazar@babylon.montreal.qc.ca

Published by:
Silver Lining
2220 Old Orchard
Montreal Qc   H4A 3A8

For Celina and Sarah, always.

Acknowledgements

These stories were first published in a slightly different form in The Gazette. I owe thanks to the many editors who have helped me over the years. Thanks in particular to Celina Segal, my ablest and dearest critic. I value the time I spend with people who make Montreal a fascinating city and who share their stories with me. Thanks to everyone on the street. You know who you are.

CONTENTS

These stories have a little something extra.

TEA WITH MR. GEORGE

Police sirens and the midday rush don't get into the Argo Book Shop. The twentieth century barely makes it past the door.

John George's Argo Book Shop is steeped in another time. There is no computer or fax machine. The cash register's highest key is marked $4. That was fine when Argo opened in 1966 and a quality paperback pocket book sold for half a buck. On the windows are poster's of Mr. George's heros: Whitman and D.H. Lawrence and Dickens. From the back you can hear the chimes of an old pendulum clock. This is not where you get cappucino and Coltrane with your Kafka.

It is a fine place for browsing though, whether you're interested in the Bhagavad-Gita or the latest Booker. But there's no Sidney Sheldon or Dick Francis on the shelves. "I've read a page or two," said Mr. George referring to the latest John Grisham, "It zips along but I don't think it's nourishing." Ahh, there you have it. Literature. Books that get one thinking. How subversive. Or, as one customer put it "I love this place. There isn't a shit book in here."

Mr. George is what may be comfortably described as senior. The nose is bulbous, the gait sometimes unsteady, but he has never needed glasses. He considered that as he brewed a pot of tea in the small back room. "I think that reading good books strengthens the eyes, do you think there's something in that?"

It is Mr. George, by the way. Talk to his friends in the trade and it's always Mr. George, the doyen of this city's book sellers.

His customers receive the same polite address. It's Professor Lucas who drops in regularly and leaves with enough time to get his next stop on the same bus transfer receipt. It's Miss Jensen who comes in to arrange a reception for a recently published book she translated. It's a courtly procession of honorifics waiting sedately in a drawer of file cards for the books they have ordered to come in.

Classics, Rodicks, Everymans, Lexis and other notable bookstores have made their marks on Montreal's literary map only to disappear. Argo has outlasted them all.

At mid-morning a woman came in and picked up Lucretius' "On the Nature of the Universe." It was $6.50. She paused and asked if it was used. "We only sell new books," said Mr. George, "but if that is too expensive there are some used book stores nearby." He started to give her addresses. She looked flustered, not expecting to hear where she could get a better deal. "No," she said, "that's okay, I'll buy this."

Shortly after the 1995 Referendum, when Quebecers voted "no" with the barest of majorities, some of Mr. George's neighbouring English language bookstore owners found their windows either smashed or sprayed with post-referendum graffiti.

Argo wasn't singled out. I thought it might be because his window is the smallest. Mr. George thinks it was probably due to the discrete selection of good French literature in the window and on his shelves. "When I opened, I wanted to have a bookstore that was half-English and half-French," he said; "but I found that I had to specialize. Still, we carry a few French books that are hard to find elsewhere."

When it first opened, Argo was the only book shop in this stretch of downtown. Now there are more than half-a-dozen, each with its specialty.

"He provided a base for others," said Terry Westcott of Westcott books, one block away. Westcott's sells used books. It compliments Argo's line of new paperbacks and hardcovers.

"I had over 3000 books in a basement apartment," he said. "One day I came home after a huge rainfall. The place had flooded and the books were ruined. I decided that if I was going to collect books, I better open a store."

Westcott learned the trade working for Mr. George. While there, he sold used books on the sidewalk. After 7 years he had enough money to start his own place.

Maybe booksellers are different, but there is something quite civilized going on here. Simon Levine, down the street at Stage Books, lost everything in a fire this summer. While he was looking for a new store, Mr. George said he could operate out of Argo. Once the new store was set up, Stage, which specializes in art and theater books, stopped selling the reference books that Argo carries. At the same time, Argo began referring it's art and architecture book customers to Stage.

Back at Argo, I asked Mr. George what he's reading these days. "Thomas Hardy," he said. "Now there was a writer who put his heart into it." From the back of the store the old clock chimed the hour. Mr. George proffered a chocolate Whippett to go with my tea. "This is a great cookie," he said. I agreed. Mr. George took another and smiled. They don't make many like that anymore.

———

I have always loved having a good book and, what they call elsewhere, a mugup. Except for colas and whiskey, liquids requires solids. My mother-in-law would no more consider having a cup of coffee or tea without a biscuit on the side than she would take her morning walk without adding a shawl to top off her sweater. It just wouldn't seem right.

Although Mr. George favours Whippets, I find them a bit rich for an every-day snack. My temperament may be more caustic and cynical than his. My flavor spectrum gravitates toward sour and bitter, tinged with sweet.

To my mind there is nothing better than ginger cookies with a glass of milk or a mug of tea or coffee. Ginger has pungency. You can't take it for granted. It pricks the tongue and makes you think. Whippets are ethereal. Light, fluffy, they are the stuff of daydreams. Ginger is rooted in earth. It's bite reminds me of where I am. Perhaps when I am older I shall look forward to a Whippet as does Mr. George. Right now, I need to be grounded as much as I can.

Here is the current version that I have been working on.

Ginger Cookies

Cream together:
1/2 cup shortening
1/2 cup blond sugar.

Add:
1 egg
1/2 cup molasses
1 tablespoon of apple cider vinegar.

Blend this well.

Sift together:
2 1/2 cups flour,
1/2 teaspoon each of baking soda,
    cloves, and nutmeg;
1/4 teaspoon each of salt and cinnamon;
1 1/4 teaspoons of ginger.

Stir the sifted ingredients into the rest.

Chill this for at least three hours.

Bake the cookies at 350°F for 5-6 min.
Makes about 50 cookies.

SERCT ISOLA

The circus is coming to town. Those six words have always thrilled me. Now I find that I share this secret passion with my six year old daughter. In this case, it is the SERCT ISOLA that she wants to see. She informed me of this by leaving a note on my desk. The letters were studiously printed next to a hand drawn picture of two smiling, stilt-walking clowns.

Here was an invitation to do something special together. Lately, I have been surprised that, except for genetic coding and constantly messy rooms, there is very little that a 45 year old man and a six year old girl really have in common. This doesn't mean that there aren't things to share, but we do have different attention spans, different perspectives. The rules always seem to shift.

Even her version of checkers can be different from mine. Young children are inherently interested in why there are rules. 45 year old men are more determined to play by them.

The gap widens when it comes to entertainment. Seeing the Lion King or reading The Cat in the Hat loses its appeal for me by the third time. Adults seek diversity. Children are comforted by the constant.

So much in their world is new. Kids are bombarded by change. They want as little of it in their lives as possible. This is one reason why a show like

Power Rangers, which we adults cannot stand, is so popular with children. The plot is invariably the same: teenagers "with attitude" and super powers defeat monsters sent from the moon to conquer earth. The show is violent in the sense that mayhem achieves results but no one dies or is seriously injured. The scripts always end the same way: the teenage heros win, the monsters disappear, and the villain gets a headache. The six o'clock television news is a far more violent and disconnected series of stories than the kids' programs which precede it.

On Power Rangers everything happens through magic – either technological wizardry for the good guys or medieval sorcery for the baddies. They are led by the notorious Rita Repulsa. Rita's gang lives on the moon where it spends most of its time creating monsters with a machine. This is part of a grand story telling tradition with Dr. Frankenstein's creation still the best of the lot.

A six year old child stands before two doors leading to our world. Both promise much, but one door is propelled by technology and the other by ineffable powers. My daughter studies both. She knows that the Power Rangers don't exist but she is willing to give Santa Claus and the Tooth Fairy a chance.

I am hesitant about pushing her in either direction. One day she is creating intricate worlds with her dolls. The next afternoon, she is playing a word game on a computer. I can watch her explorations. I can even enter her worlds to a limited extent but they remain hers.

That is why the circus is so wonderful. It is an arena for magic that she and I equally appreciate. It is a world of wonders, where people must work together to achieve perfection. It is a medium for real virtuosos rather than virtual realities.

It is, of course, as impossible a world for either of us to join as the world of the Power Rangers, but that doesn't stop us from laughing at the clowns or holding our breaths as acrobats and trapeze artists balance above us.

The world of the circus is sensuous. My memories were formed with the smells and sights from my first visit. I was five and went to the Ringling Brothers, Barnum and Bailey's "Greatest Show on Earth." Before the show, I walked through the sideshow. My small hand patted the leg of shackled elephants. I talked with giants and bearded ladies. That's all gone. The Greatest Show on Earth's carnival was too expensive too maintain. Even if that wasn't so, it would be killed today as politically correct.

At 22, I briefly considered joining a small circus as it traveled through upstate New York but a contortionist warned me that I'd be cleaning up after the elephants and could do that for years.

My daughter carries her own image of what a circus should be. It is one of smiling stilt-walking clowns, of fun and magic that she can't explain and I won't decipher. There is so little in what the world offers her, particularly on television, that is either really wonderful or full of wonder. Both she and I risk becoming jaded and cynical. I know that soon she'll even find the Power Rangers boring, but the SERCT ISOLA (which others call the Cirque du Soleil) is insidious. A little bit opens the mind to the impossible and that is good for the soul.

The all time favourite circus food has got to be

popped corn. There are few specialty appliances in our kitchen, but I do have an old two quart pot with a good lid that I use only for this. I use popping corn that I buy by the kilo from a health food store bin. It's cheaper and tastier than a microwave popcorn pack.

I make the popcorn in small batches. I heat up the pot and pour two tablespoons of vegetable or peanut oil and add a small pat of butter. It always takes a lot longer to heat up the pot for the first batch. When the butter is sizzling, I add a third of a cup of popcorn, just enough to cover the base of the pot. I cover it and wait until for the first kernel to pop. Then I shake the pot like crazy over the heat, using two hands, one for the handle and the other to keep the lid tight. When I hear no more popping, I dump the popped corn into a large brown paper bag, salt the corn and shake it up. Excess grease gets absorbed by the bag. I keep popping corn until I have as much in the bag as I want. Some people like to top it off with a little cheddar cheese or paprika or garlic powder or flakes of chili. I like it simple. Salt and the butter from the popping as the corn gods intended.

SPRING AT THE BORDER

Monday June 5 was a glorious day. In Montreal, gardens were becoming lush. The farms between here and the US border were loamed with rich black earth and the green of new growth.

This was our first hot day and it had that mad twist of the seasons which Montrealers take for granted. It was a day with more summer in it than spring. My wife, who knew central Europe as a child, says that we don't know what spring is. And she is right. In Europe, it is gradual. There, the seasons each last a full three months. They evolve as nature intended, in a constant nurturing rhythm.

Here spring is an accident, less a season than a meteorological faultline. We take off our coats and call that spring. A week later the airconditioning goes on. Nevertheless, June 5 was a glorious day.

It was a glorious day at the border too. There is a small white trailer on the Canadian side of the demarcation separating Champlain, New York from St-Bernard-de-Lacolle, Quebec. The trailer has no sign. It is informally called the white house. If you drive by it, as thousands do every day, you would likely think it a construction trailer. It is as anonymous as it is intended, as the people who are inside. This is where those claiming to be refugees wait until an immigration officer gives them permission to enter Canada. If they get permission it is only the start of the process; full refugee status may be years later.

As the sun rose on June 5, a man from Bangladesh was waiting in the white house. Across from him was a young couple from Honduras. They had spent weeks getting this far.

The man from Honduras spoke softly. He had been in a union. There was a protest against the government. He and the woman were fleeing for their lives. She was two months pregnant.

At about the same time, further away, a Russian family was about to leave the Port Authority Bus Terminal in New York City and get on a bus to Plattsburg. They had been victims, a minority on the wrong side of an undeclared war somewhere in the former USSR. Two days ago they left Moscow for New York. Now they were coming here.

It's easy to get a tourist visa to the USA, hard to get one for Canada. It's easier to claim refugee status in Canada, harder to do that in the USA. The bus had taken them from New York City. The driver left them in Plattsburg. A taxi would get them to the border. Everyone knows the rules. If you don't, you can pay someone to tell you. Someone promises to take care of the problem and it will only cost all you have.

The man from Bangladesh said that he had spent the last 30 hours travelling. He said that he had fled at the last minute. Political problems. He had paid a broker $10,000. The broker said that he would arrange everything and get him into Canada. The two of them had flown together from Bangladesh to New York City. In New York the broker had taken his papers and passport and put him on a bus to Plattsburg. Where was the broker that had promised to bring him into Canada? A shrug. What can you do?

The father of a Pakistani family said that he had paid 800,000 rupees to get this far, to the white house. That's about $40,000 for a family of four. Someone else said that the going rate in Sri Lanka was $20,000 a person.

The man from Pakistan came with his wife and two children. Their faces were flushed with a redness that is the tiredness at the other end of fatigue. This is a tiredness that comes from three days of constant travelling without any guarantee of a haven; a tiredness that finally shows as they wait in the white house.

"Esperamos," said the man from Honduras. It means "we wait" and yet, in Spanish it also means "we hope."

The sun set at 8:39 P.M. on Monday, June 5. A little earlier, a Greyhound bus heading to Montreal had stopped at the border. At Lacolle, passengers enter Canada through a special boarding area. They disembark, go through customs and get back on the bus.

If there is room, the driver can take on additional passengers for the final leg to Montreal. That evening a young man from Honduras and his wife got on. So did a man from Bangladesh. There would be later buses throughout the night and others, from other countries, would get on.

The man from Honduras smiled through his exhaustion. "Esperamos," he had said. It was a glorious day after all.

TWO ALARM CHICKEN

In my neighbourhood, the rites of spring don't start with the sighting of the first robin or the budding of huge silver maples that line our street. My neighbours know that winter is officially over when smoke billows from the Lazar balcony.

This is an ignominious distinction which I share with other male members of my clan. As far as I can tell, Lazar men have been burning large pieces of meat over outdoor fire-pits for generations. It would not surprise me if future discoveries of prehistoric cave paintings show a Lazar searing his fingers with a haunch of Jurassic brisket held inexpertly over glowing coals. To be accurate, the painting would also show him attacking the meat with a long handled basting brush. Nearby, would be a gourd of secret sauce.

This is what it is all about, the basics of survival: fire, food and an innate ability to cover up the acrid taste of charred meat with several layers of carmelized muck.

Barbecue has an unclear etymology. Some say it comes from the Spanish "barbacoa" which is a raised platform used to keep an ox or sheep above the flames. Others think it's a French idiom to describe roasting an animal from "la barbe à la queue" (from the beard to the tail). The female members of my family believe that no matter it's roots, the word really means "look at what that idiot is doing now."

Barbecuing is a deeply primal activity. There could be other, subconscious reasons why men are intuitively drawn to cooking outside the kitchen. These may include a return to nature, the sensual pleasure of working with ones hands, and the gratification of providing sustenance for friends and family. While important, these are secondary to the fundamental reason for barbecuing: playing with fire.

Great barbecue chefs know that this is what it is all about. Paul Prudhomme, master Cajun chef and originator of the all-time-greatest-playing-with-fire meal, "blackened redfish," understands this. Word for word, here is how the recipe for this truly magnificent dish begins. "Heat a large cast-iron skillet over very high heat until it is beyond the smoking stage and you see white ash in the skillet bottom (the skillet cannot be too hot for this dish), at least ten minutes."

Now, that's cooking.

My own claim to membership in the Barbecuing Hall of Fame rests with what is locally known as "two-alarm chicken."

Before I tell you how to make this unique dish, you should know that the Second Annual Weber Canadian Barbecue Survey found that successful barbecuing secrets include "using wood chips" and "cooking slowly on low heat with the lid down." Among the most common mistakes, is "constantly lifting the barbecue lid to check the coals and the food while it's cooking."

With this in mind, I lit the fire and, once the coals were ready, added a few chunks of apple wood to give the chicken a smoky flavor. I covered the grill and went inside the house to do some work.

Soon after, one of the family heard walkie talkies outside. Looking down from the balcony, we noticed the helmets, yellow overcoats and axes which distinguish fire fighters from, say, telephone company repairmen.

I ran to the balcony as two hook and ladder trucks pulled up to the house. I lifted the hood off the barbecue and, with gloved hands, held an impressively carbonized bird over the balcony railing for all to see. I thought this gave the scene an heroic touch, much as Caesar might have done, had he bestowed barbecued chicken instead of laurels upon the crowd below.

To their credit, the firemen put down their hoses and cheered. One of them came upstairs. He asked about the kitchen smoke detector which at that time was doubling as a hat rack. He told me to give the fire department a warning call the next time I made a barbecue.

There is no recipe for great barbecue. There is only trial and error. There is heat and passion and the exquisite sense of timing that lets you know when the smoked chicken or barbecued ribs are ready. The slower the better. Barbecue is to summer what beer is to barbecue.

Put the meat on a slow cooking, covered barbecue, and keep the temperature between 180° and 250°F . It should take about a six pack, that's a beer an hour, to do it right.

My inspiration for my approach to barbecue, and living graciously in general, comes from a wonderful newsletter called "Simple Cooking" by John Thorne and Matt Lewis Thorne. *(They can be reached at matt&john@outlawcook.com.)*

This recipe will work for both ribs and chicken.

BBQ

For the rub:
6 cloves of garlic
2 tablespoons of sea salt
To taste:
cayenne, chili pepper, freshly ground black pepper, cumin (at least a teaspoon of each)
some olive oil

For the mop:
one onion, chopped fine
1/4 cup olive oil
1/8 teaspoon each salt and pepper
1 cup of cider vinegar
1 cup of beer

For the sop:
Your favorite commercial barbecue sauce
or 1/2 cup of ketchup added to left over mop

Split the chicken down the back. Turn it over (skin up) and flatten it out with your hands. If using ribs, remove as much fat layered on top as is easily possible.

Prepare the rub by crushing the garlic into a paste with the salt. Add the rest of the spices and enough oil to make it smooth but not liquid.

With your hands, massage the rub into the meat. Let it sit covered, overnight, in the refrigerator.

To prepare the mop, dice the onion well and cook it slowly in the oil. When it becomes translucent, add the cider and beer. Bring this to a boil and reduce the heat to a simmer for about 10 minutes. Store in the refrigerator.

The next day start the fire before noon. If using coals, you'll need a full pan. If using a gas barbecue with a smoking attachment, bring it up to about 350°F and then reduce it to about 225°F when you put the meat in.

In either case, do not have the meat in contact with the flames. Either separate it with a water bath, or rack the coals to one side of the pan, or only use one burner of a gas grill. The key is long slow cooking with no flare ups.

When the fire is ready add the smoking chips (apple or maple are best) and the meat. Check the heat every hour, adjusting it and adding coals as necessary. Baste it with the mop at the same time.

Baste with barbecue sauce for the last 15 minutes or so but not much longer because the tomato or sugar in the sauce may carmelize and burn.

DORVAL ISLAND

This fantasy comes in summer. It's about vacations with quiet walks outdoors and summer camping, and a cottage where the screen door slams as kids run through the kitchen in wet bathing suits. It's a fantasy that includes barbecues, forests and water. There are heady sensations in these fantasies. They're the smells of cedar and pine, scrabbling on dirt paths, and the cool touch of waves and wind.

I wondered if I had found my fantasy when I saw the realtor's notice: "Join the very few who call this gorgeous paradise 'home'." Paradise was fifteen minutes from downtown Montreal, in Canada's smallest city, Dorval Island.

The City of Dorval Island is a short ferry ride from the City of Dorval, but most Montrealers probably don't know much about it. Both municipalities were named after Jean Bouchard d'Orval, a fur trader who bought the land in 1692.

The island's local historian, Betty Locke, says that the Sulpicians likely used it as an Indian school in 1667. There is evidence that, a couple of years later, the Iroquois made it their base for assaults on the fur trading community in Lachine.

In the 19th century, Sir George Simpson, governor of the Hudson's Bay Company and locally known as "the emperor of Lachine," bought the island for a summer home. He entertained family, clients, and visitors there. Queen Victoria's son, the

Prince of Wales, was once paddled over.

In 1910, the island ended up in the hands of a local land syndicate. The group was going to create an amusement park. Dorval City residents were opposed and the park never got beyond the plans. The syndicate then decided to get its money out by creating a watery suburbia with "boats, bathing, beaches…" The prospectus showed places for several hundred homes and waterfront lots going for 20 cents a square foot.

Perhaps it was the inaccessibility. Perhaps it was the depression of the 1930s. In the end, a few dozen lots were sold. Today there are 58 homes with room for no more.

Stepping on to the island today is both difficult and a revelation. Attitudes haven't changed a lot since it was Sir George's private preserve. The public notice he sent around in 1885 – "that … no person is at liberty to land there except by authority from my agent" is pretty much the case today.

Ask the boatman if you can visit and he'll likely say "no, not unless you know someone." Gisèle Chapleau, mayor of Dorval Island, says that while it is not illegal to come here (remember this is a part of the Montreal Urban Community) the town does its best to discourage the uninvited. There are no welcome signs, no stores, no public beaches, no services, no cars, not even a paved road.

What there is, is constancy. In a world where change is congruent with chaos, here is a town that has held its own for 80 years. You'd have to be around a long time to see anything new. The cedars which were once harvested for firewood have been replaced by ash and poplar. Many of the large cottages, built in the 1930s, have been handed down through generations. They are unchanged and immaculately maintained.

There are only a few modern intrusions. Electricity came to the island in 1950. The community swimming pool was built in 1960 "when Lake St. Louis became Lake Sewage," says one resident.

Still, it's easy to succumb to the past. The bicycles next to the ferry dock are left unlocked. Corn roasts are still held near the town hall. A workman puts up cedar shingles to make a recently built shed look old.

If you want excitement, or groceries, you can always take the boat across the water. "That's the way we like it," says Locke, who has been coming here every summer since 1930. She points to the city's shield made up of a maple leaf, fleur de lys and a tree. Underneath it is the motto, in pax tranquilitate.

So it's a surprise to find that this summer fantasy of mine is best left in the past. It may be that there is too much paradise here. "No poison ivy, no dogs off leash," said the mayor. More brutally, for the boy from the city, it's too quiet here.

You can hear birds, the wind in the trees, maybe even a thought drop. After a couple of hours, I realized I wasn't ready for it. I could see myself coming down to the dock in the evening just to catch the sound of traffic on highway 20. After an afternoon of bliss, I yearned for the pulse of downtown. I got back on the ferry and enjoyed the diesel fumes all the way home.

FEAR

The night before the referendum, I went for a walk and found fear. It was the fear that comes with impotence and bad endings. It was out there as fragile as autumn. Not quite an end in itself, but coming to an end. A couple of nights ago, that slightly mawkish feeling forced me out of the house. It was a moment to savour, to become a walker in the city and enjoy what we have.

I can tell you that I am not alone. There are many walkers in the city and the walk is different for each of us. We are alone without being lonely. That night, the walk took me to Momesso's in the few blocks of Little Italy that's left on Upper Lachine road.

Momesso's serves the best sausage sub in the city. It's also got great espresso and good grappa. This is one hell of a combination but I knew it would take my mind off the fear that was building inside, off the panic that had registered from conversations I had heard all week. No politics tonight, just big screens showing a hockey game and a few innings of Cleveland sticking it to the Braves.

A walker in the city sees things differently at night and I have to walk to really sense what's there. Going to a downtown bar makes me feel ebullient or panicky. Sometimes both rush into the system together. It's like a beer and a shot punching it out. There was something out there. To find it, I had to go beyond the clubs and bars.

I knew I wasn't going to find it driving around in a car. Driving's as powerful a drug as any other. A car encases the body and the mind. It isoaltes and insulates and it takes you away.

Still, it was tempting. It would be so easy to open the throttle and cruise from the fear and panic and the moment. But eventually, I would return and what ever I was running from would still be there. So I became a walker in the city and I walked and watched and listened. I heared foosteps coming from behind and one fear supplanted another.

I turned, but not too quickly. It was a woman, leaving her home and walking to a bus stop down the street. No one bothered her. A little while later I watched a mother walk into Momesso's and get a coffee to go. She had her baby bundled and cradled in an arm. No one payed her any special attention. She didn't seem worried about walking back to her place late at night. In so many ways, it's a good city.

I walked by two large billboards. One for the No side, the other for Yes. "Forts, Fiers, Ensemble" said the first. "… ça devient possible" cried the second. The signs were so well lit that they blocked out the stars. The wind blew hard against the billboards. They echoed as two beats of a bass drum, each irrelevant but for the other.

I walked knowing that walking would change nothing. I paused in a doorway on Sherbrooke street to read a notice about an advance poll. It had served it's purpose days ago.

I had wandered into Westmount and stumbled across unexpected optimism. A few days before the end of the world, someone had opened a store selling only teddy bears. A few blocks further, a brother and sister had started a snack bar that featured fresh fruit compotes. A large red faced man gripping a bottle in a brown paper bag got my attention. He yelled "I'm the greatest" and smiled.

Who is more deluded? Is it me caught by a fear of the unknown? Is it young entrepreneurs opening up new stores in Westmount days before the vote? Or is it a man who wanders the streets and thinks he's swell?

Then there are the delusions we've come to accept as normal. A friend says her "oui" will help Quebec get what it needs. I think it may cleave the country. We both read the same question but each thinks the other doesn't understand what is going on. For the moment, we suffer each other's "delusions" gracefully and, in the end, fear the consequences of each other's action.

KLEZ

Every once in a while, if you're lucky, you can see the the pattern shift and the stereotypes dissolve.

Most of the time that doesn't happen. Most of the time, it's easier to make assumptions where there is only illusion. So we split the city along the Main or pretend that every issue has three sides: franco, anglo, and allo. We use the terms so readily that we forget what they mean. We forget that a label doesn't represent reality.

With this in mind, I give you the group Shirim Klezmer. Klezmer music goes back hundreds of years. It was played by Jewish itinerants on street corners, at weddings and community celebrations. This is buskers' music. It uses easily carried instruments: accordions, trumpets and clarinets, with room for a tub-thumping bass and, always, a fiddler on the roof. Watch any cartoon from the fifties and you'll hear the syncopated ragtime of klezmer music. Listen to a recording with Benny Goodman's clarinet or the opening of Gershwin's "Rhapsody in Blue" and you'll hear the plaintiff cry of a Jewish soul.

Shirim Klezmer was in town recently. The band rips the klezmer stereotype to shreds. This is traditional Eastern European Jewish folk music brought to the outer reaches of jazz, old roots fused to tone poems, Benny Goodman fine-tuned by Joe Cocker.

The leader of Shirim Klezmer is Glenn Dickson, a nice non-Jewish guy from Virginia. So much for another stereotype. But, if you don't have to be Italian to sing opera, why should you be Jewish to compose klez?

The singer is Betty Silberman from Montreal. Here is someone who grew up in Côte-des-Neiges, went to Northmount High and left for Boston more than 20 years ago.

Another stereotype shatters. Silberman talks to the crowd in French. Young, transplanted "anglo-Montrealers" are supposed to forget their roots, but Silberman has stayed trilingual. "I had French friends and spoke Yiddish at home," she said, "I never dreamed that I would have spent the past seven years with a klezmer band or that I would do a cabaret act in Boston nightclubs with Yiddish songs."

The stereotype also says that a klezmer concert must take place in a Jewish neighbourhood, Côte-St-Luc maybe; certainly not to a sell-out local crowd in the east-end's Maison de la culture Frontenac.

"Ahh," says René Moisan, the show's promoter, "the audience at this concert was definitely not Jewish but they loved the music." Moisan runs Productions Bros, an agency that books over a hundred music acts each year. These are folk, world-beat and blues groups. He says that Montreal's festivals have helped us develop broader cultural tastes. "Montrealers are more open to others now. Music is a great way to appreciate culture."

Something is happening here and if you stay with the stereotype, you'll be lost. A few people were disappointed at the concert. They had come expecting a standard Yiddish repertoire, classic songs done in a familiar style. Some wanted high stepping hora dances and Shirim Klezmer did play a few of those.

For the most part, the group "pushed the envelope," as Dickson said. "We are using a modern harmonic structure. We haven't decided where we are going." A few couldn't follow and left, but hundreds stayed to the end, gave the group three standing ovations, and yelled for more. Who would have thought that an evening of Yiddish music protruding through improvisational jazz would have so many fans?

So much has changed, and not just in music. Silberman who returns here often to visit her family, says that this is a different city, even from the one she grew up in. "Montreal is pretty incredible. It is very progressive. There is an organic quality and an openness to enjoy life." Again, another stereotype shattered. So much for the prevailing focus that we are a narrow-minded, dismal society which has exchanged its joie-de -vivre for Maalox.

Sometimes it takes an outsider to let you know that you've got a good thing.

One of Shirim's last songs at the concert was "Lomir zeh iberbeiten." It means "Let's make up." The original song is about two people getting together after a fight but Silberman added new verses in French for this show. She sang of nations making peace and people coming together. She made sure that the audience understood every word.

LOYALISTS

I told a friend that I was going to a meeting of the United Empire Loyalists. "They still exist?" he said.

United Empire Loyalists are descended from the American colonists who were loyal to the British during the American revolution. Theirs was a mixed group of refugees. It included British, Germans, Swiss, French, Dutch, Blacks, Jews, Italians, and Mohawks. The United Empire Loyalist shield has 13 swords and a tomahawk protecting a crown. Above this are a brown arm and a white arm jointly raising the Union Jack.

About 50 thousand Loyalists fled into Canada. Their impact was immediate and enduring. New Brunswick was split off from Nova Scotia to accommodate them. Ontario, then called Upper Canada, was separated from Quebec for the same reason.

Undoubtedly, Canada would have have been different if the Loyalists hadn't fled north. Of course, there would not have been a revolution if the British hadn't given special rights, in 1774, to the French speaking, Catholic inhabitants of their newest colony – Quebec. Well, that's the kind of argument Loyalists still have.

Today the Association has about 3000 members across the country. 50 are in Montreal. United Empire Loyalists have the right to put UE after their names. They remember that the quotation which begins as "Je me souviens" ends with "grew up under the lily and flourished under the rose."

Loyalists know their roots. The association's officers include a genealogist. They are the other souche.

About 60 people showed up for the annual meeting of the Montreal chapter – the Heritage Branch of the United Empire Loyalists' Association of Canada. . There were representatives of other organizations as well, such as the St. David's Society, the Monarchist League, the Fraser Highlanders Regiment, and the English Speaking Union of Quebec. A member of Alliance Quebec was there too. He said he was looking for new members for his organization.

Col. the Honourable John R. Matheson, O.C., K.St.J., C.D., Q.C., U.E. gave the keynote speech. He spoke passionately about why Canada needs Quebec. He talked of the "creative tension" between Quebec and Canada that fosters national virtues of accommodation, passion, and tolerance. He finished by quoting a French poem he had written many years ago. One of the lines was "Malgré nous, nous sommes unis." (In spite of ourselves, we are together).

Andrew Cook-Jolicoeur was also there. His blazer sported an elegant Fraser Highlanders regimental crest with the motto in old French "Je suis prest." (I am ready). Mr. Cook-Jolicoeur traces his family's arrival to just after the founding of Quebec City. He works as a translator and speaks fluent German and French. His English is brushed with Gaelic. "I am a chameleon," he said.

Mr. Cook-Jolicoeur is 39. He is proud of his ancestry, proud to be Canadian.

"We're not pure laîne," he said. "No one is 100

per cent this, that or the other thing. It's a fantasy. Let's try to find common ground instead of looking for areas where we disagree.

"This country is worth fighting for. Not worth fighting for with a sword," he quickly added, "but to make a stand and say this is an important country. I don't want to lose what my ancestors worked for."

Mr. Cook-Jolicoeur introduced me to Adrian Willison. Mr. Willison is 41 and is thinking of joining the UEL. He is getting his lineage in order. Mr. Willison was wearing a Quebec tartan tie.

The Quebec tartan is a red, blue and green plaid cross-barred with narrow bands of white and gold. Mr. Cook-Jolicoeur said that each of the colours refers to different elements of Quebec's shield. The green is for maple leaves, the gold and blue for the fleur-de-lis, the red for the lion and the crown. This is known as a district tartan. All Quebecers can wear it.

Mr. Cook-Jolicoeur is hoping that Quebecers can commemorate "la vieille alliance" of France and Scotland during Tartan Day which is April 6. Canada and each province and territory all have distinctive tartans. Tartan Day was recently officially celebrated in five provinces, Quebec was not one of them.

Loyalists say their organization is not an anachronism. They believe it has something to offer, a way to enhance our national esteem. "Regardless of what our backgrounds are, we are Canadians," said Mr. Cook-Jolicoeur. "We are patriots. This is a wonderful country."

At the end of the meeting everyone was invited to sing "our national anthem and our royal anthem." O Canada was sung in the usual fragmented form with occasional lines of French woven through the English. Most people fumbled a bit to get to the end. Everyone knew the words to God Save the Queen.

THE RESTAURANT WITH NO NAME

The restaurant at the end of the universe has no name and no menu. It only serves lunch. It was a gift from the king of the mushrooms to his son.

The son of the king of the mushrooms was mystified. We had brought him mushrooms from the lawn of a friend. We thought they were edible but no one remembered what they were called. We brought ours, with their large white caps and thick stems still attached to clumps of grass, here, to the restaurant with no name on boulevard St-Michel, at the edge of Montreal.

The mushroom king, Antonio Totarella, is retired. He came here from Italy in 1963 and started working at a bottling factory. He made $45 a week. "I looked around and said, you can make a job in Canada for yourself." He worked at the Marché Central. He put some money together, found a truck, and started bringing in common table mushrooms from Hamilton. "The first three months I lost $8000. There were too many on the market. Then the market changed and I made money." A few years ago Totarella sold his company and bought his son, Louis, a small restaurant.

The king of the mushrooms had hoped that his son might take over the business but Louis had more exotic ideas. He showed me a commercial, glass-door refrigerator at one end of the restaurant. I could see a few dozen bottles of beer, a plate of grilled and marinated red peppers, some cantaloups, a box of figs, and a jar filled with rice. On top of the rice were knobby black golf balls.

Louis opened the jar. The golf balls smelled of autumn in the woods, old port, and roasted chestnuts. "These are black truffles from Umbria," he said. "$600 a kilo. I had some white ones in last week. They sold for $2100 a kilo."

Louis sliced one open. He pointed to a webbing of white running through the thick black core. "This is tuber estivo – we call it the poor man's truffle." He put the truffle back in the jar. He didn't offer me a slice.

Mushrooms are everywhere in the restaurant with no name. There are bags of mushroom powder, dried cepes and morels, a mushroom statue, and posters of edible and inedible fungi on the wall. A television was on when we entered. The Fresh Prince of Bel-Air was talking about food. I heard him say "It's good. Just add cream of mushroom soup."

Louis picked up my bag of lawn mushrooms. "Smells nice, could be a pleurote." This was good news. The best known of the pleurotes is the oyster mushroom. It's a delicacy. 5 Saisons sells them for almost $30 a kilo. I noticed that Louis had a box of oyster mushrooms on the bottom of his fridge. They didn't look like mine. "Hmm," he said after a little more study. "I'll call Sergio."

Exotic mushrooms are big business. Louis buys them from Europe, Nova Scotia, the Western USA and Canada. Most varieties are wild and picked by hand. Louis says that mushroom lovers in Japan pay up to $2000 a kilo for a plate of Canadian grown matsutake. Another variety that was $6 a kilo wholesale last year now costs him $80.

There's a large jar of mushrooms on the counter. It's packed with almost 1000 marinated bolete mushrooms. Italians call them porcini. The jar sells for $3000. Louis thinks that no one will ever eat them. "It's like an expensive bottle of wine," he said. "It will look good in a fancy restaurant."

Sergio arrived. I asked him to look at my mushrooms, but they had disappeared. Antonio was cooking them. Sergio found a small uncooked piece and examined it. "You find it on a tree?" he asked. "No," I said, "it was on the lawn." "I cannot help you," he said. "I look for mushrooms in the forest. That is my specialty. You sure it wasn't on wood?"

The son of the mushroom king told us to sit down. He brought over a book, Mushrooms Demystified. Wild mushrooms are hard to identify. Some taste great, some can kill you. Most are somewhere in between. "Here's a good one," Louis said. "You won't die but you'll vomit like crazy."

The king of the mushrooms came to the table. My lawn mushrooms smelled wonderful. Good olive oil and garlic will do that. He brought over thin slices of pecorino cheese laced with truffles. Not bad. He put a thimble sized jar of truffle olive oil on the table to dot our bread. He carted out dishes of penne with wild mushrooms and a mound of braised chanterelles.

As we ate, Antonio told us that the restaurant has no name because they once put up a sign but didn't have a permit for the sign. "I had to pay a fine. I did it again but it wasn't the right size and I paid another fine. So we said that's all right. So the restaurant has no name."

Louis didn't join us. "I don't eat mushrooms anymore," he said. Never? "The only one I eat is the white truffle. Sometimes, I go to a good restaurant and tell the chef, 'please, cook me this'."

———

After all this, I had to put a mushroom recipe in the book. Here's the easiest one I know. Find someone who knows how to forage for young pleurotes or puff-balls. If you don't know what you've got, forget it. Look for fresh oyster mushrooms in the fancy produce section of the supermarket. Wash and clean the mushrooms, dry them and then slice them to the width of your finger. Toss them in a bag that has a cup of flour and several shakes of salt and pepper. In a frying pan, heat some olive oil and a little butter until the butter is briskly bubbling. Shake off the excess flour and fry the mushrooms quick and crisp. Remove the mushrooms to a hot plate in the oven. Deglaze the pan with a good squeeze of lemon and add that to the mushrooms. Think twice about inviting the neighbours. This is good.

———

EATING SEAL

The first question you will not have is about the wine; but it was one that occurred to me after I left Réjean Lachapelle's butcher shop, Gival, in the Atwater market with a quarter kilo of fresh seal meat.

After all, seal is a dark meat, as black and shiny as anthracite, so red wine seems appropriate. On the other hand, it comes from the sea, so white wine with sea food, no?

But that is probably not the question you are asking yourself now.

First, you may be surprised that fresh seal meat is available in Montreal. Réjean has it regularly. Last week he had a shipment from his wife's home, in Iles de la Madeleine.

Gival is a specialty butcher shop. That's what the sign says on the market wall. The word "specialty" when adjacent to the word "butcher" should set off a little warning bell. In Quebec, it is often code for a seller of horse meat.

Gival sells horse; and also grain fed chickens, smoked lamb, boar paté, terrines of bison mixed with crushed oranges and cranberries, their own smoked salmon – just what you'd expect if Radisson and des Groseillers were your neighbourhood purveyors.

In this company, seal isn't a total surprise, but I wouldn't expect to see it at Provigo soon. Gival sells it for $27.99 a kilo, near the elk steaks ($64.99 a kilo) and caribou ($40.00 a kilo). At those prices the blueberry and wild boar sausages ($1.79 a piece) look like a bargain.

Frankly, a small amount of game goes a long way. This is meat with an intense flavor and little or no fat. Seal has the texture of steak and tastes like mild beef liver. It's not bad fried with onions, grinds up nicely for meat balls to simmer in a spicy tomato sauce, and holds its shape in a basic Iles de la Madelaine four root (onions, carrots, potatoes, and turnip) stew.

The black colour is a magnificent counterpoint to the red of the tomato sauce or the subtle orange, gold and white of the vegetables. Nature has provided for an incredible spectrum of food colours but black is sorely lacking. Purely from aesthetics, seal meat makes for an unusual addition to the table. However, this was probably not what you were thinking of either.

You might be wondering "why would he eat the stuff?" I could answer "in the interests of science" or that "this is the type of important investigative inquiry for which journalists enter the profession." This is all, of course, true; but I did not do it merely in the interests of science and The Gazette does not have "Lazar will eat seal meat" in my contract.

And it is not just because I am worried that the economy will not survive unless we support Canadian industries and our natural resources. There are abysmally few jobs for those in eastern Quebec and the Maritimes. Inuit could use the income and Newfoundlanders are facing another fishless year. Why not help a great many people by switching to a diet of nutritious, no fat seal meat?

Seal, a favorite of Inuit, the meat that could ease Maritimers out of the UIC line, a dish that is less dangerous to our national health than turbot is about to make the jump from "bas" to "haute" cuisine. When this happens, a fundamental question will have to be answered.

In the interests of science and to help the economy, I can now tell you the answer. It's not bad with white and it's fine with a full-bodied red; but it is perhaps most memorable as it was once served to me in Newfoundland, with copious amounts of extremely potent rum.

TONY THE KNIFE SHARPENER

You always hear the knife sharpener before you see him. He starts ringing the bell on his truck at the top of the block. It's a rebuilt Canada Post van painted orange. The words "Aiguisage Tony – Tony's Sharpening" are scripted in black across the sides.

You can stand on the street and try to spot the van, just to make sure it's him; but that doesn't give you enough time go back in and get the knives that need to be sharpened. Besides, no one wants to come running down the stairs with a handful of knives, even if they are dull. You know what they say, "the dull ones are always the most dangerous." So the best way to catch the truck is to hear it first.

These days, Carmine drives. He is at least the third generation of his family to do this. I say "at least" because his family is from Campobasso in Italy. "Everyone there sharpened knives," he said. "They'd go out to the other villages and work. In another town, everyone might repair shoes or do something else, but everyone in Campobasso sharpened knives.

"My grandfather came over and worked in construction. Whenever he got laid off he'd go around, carrying what he needed on his back. Then he got a cart. Then we got a truck. Tony's my father. He worked in construction and did this too.

"We used to live in Cornwall. We'd come to Montreal and go down the streets; but there are more houses on Montreal streets than in Cornwall, so we moved here. My father doesn't come out now too often.

"I may be the last in my family to do this. People throw away everything. Shoes lose their heels, knives get dull. A guy will just get a new one. I'm from the old generation. We repaired everything.

"Besides, who wants this kind of job. Well, maybe these days. At least it's a job. I like it because I can work my own hours, go where I want. Dollard one day, NDG the next. I go anywhere. I stop when I want.

"A couple of times a year somebody brings me a sword. It's just going to hang in the living room but they want it to look nice."

Carmine grinds anything. He takes a knife, a pair of scissors, an axe, a chisel and sets them to the stones. He once took the dents out of a spoon which had fallen into a kitchen garburator. The smaller grindstones are on the right of the truck. The big gasoline powered motor on the left runs a long lathe that was built more than a hundred years ago. It's set up for lawnmowers.

I show Carmine our mower. It's a manual one. We have a small lawn; it shouldn't take long to cut. But the blades are dull, the mower hasn't been cleaned in years. Carmine starts his big gas engine. He takes a strong jerk of a hand-pulled starter. One pull. The rope comes out a couple of feet and the engine roars. He takes off the long handle from the mower and pokes out the grass and dirt trapped along the edges. He removes the covers from the mower's wheels and sprays the gears with WD-40. "I use this stuff by the gallon," he says, "but it's evaporates too quickly." He takes an oil can and squirts engine oil over everything.

He cradles the body of the mower between a pair of steel bars and oils another bar, parallel to the first two, along which a big grindstone spins.

The sound of stone shearing metal is painful. It is the sound of the worst dentist in the world. It is the sound of an endless screech, of an accident waiting to happen. To Carmine it's merely loud. He moves slowly, delicately reshaping the face of each curved blade against the abrading stone. The rust peels off leaving a clean sheen of steel along the edge. Sparks arc across the truck. A boy crosses the street to watch from the door open at the back.

This is something old, a craft practiced since stone was exchanged for bronze. Yet for the child this is new. There is a raw power in the sharpener's hand that is seldom seen outside a factory, certainly not on a residential street.

Carmine sets the blade and finishes his work. The mower turns well but not as easily as he wants. He makes adjustments and adds oil. Finally he apologizes that there must be some dirt that he cannot reach. It doesn't matter. The mower runs through the long grass like a scythe.

And Carmine's knives? He has a rack of them for sale in the back of the truck. The handles are battered but the blades are ready. At home, it's another story. "You know how it is," he says, "the shoemaker's kids go barefoot... and the knife sharpener's knives are always a little dull."

URBAN HARVEST

It's been a good harvest for the urban forager. I was reminded of this when we returned home late one evening. It was almost midnight.The car was full of luggage and there was a sleeping child to haul upstairs. But first things first. Our neighbours popped out of their kitchen with spoonfuls of just made grape jam. The first batch of CP '95 was ready.

These jams and jellies are part of neighbourhood lore. The grapes came from our local cornucopia-de-quartier. They had been picked that afternoon from wild vines growing by the Canadian Pacific railroad tracks, along de Maisonneuve boulevard west.

This year's batch was sweet but not cloying. It had a touch of astringency that might have come from bitter seeds still in the pulp. All in all, I thought it was a better batch than last year's but not quite as full bodied as the memorable CP '88. That was the first time we took part in the local harvest. I seem to remember that that particular batch had a distinct tang. Perhaps the trains packed a little more diesel in their exhaust back then.

The brush next to the tracks yields more than grapes. This is a narrow wedge of countryside along a major traffic route. It's untamed land, three kilometres long and only a couple of metres wide, running along a poorly maintained fence from the

Vendome Metro station to the Montreal West commuter rail stop.

The brush has trees, bushes, sometimes a small swamp. An asphalt cycling path separates it from the traffic. This path is also used by dog walkers, joggers, and the occasional urban forager. Heard about multi-tasking environments? Here's a splendid example of how many people, with different interests, put a small bit of the city to good use.

The brush is cut once or twice a year but is generally left pretty much alone. It's a long, thin swath of urban anarchy. Unlike the mountain or other semi-wilderness areas in the city, the land next to the tracks is ripe for harvest. In early summer, food pickers come for milkweed shoots and dandelion leaves. By August, flower pickers are gathering bouquets of yarrow, sunflowers and day lilies.

The wild grape vines yield four seasons of abundance. In late spring and early summer there are leaves for Greek dolmas. In the fall there are grapes. Before Christmas, the bare vines are culled for wreaths.

Standing on the overpass at Grand and de Maisonneuve, there's a palette of fall colours along the tracks. Purple Virginia creeper and leafy red sumac grow along the fences bordering the tracks. Pink prairie mallow and purple asters stand out among the uncut brush. A small grove of swamp grass stands above the passing cars. The grasses have long, rush-like stems and thick, lacy brown tassels.

The overpass does more than link two sides of Grand boulevard over the rail tracks. Communities cross here. The large, two-storey high concrete walkway is a signpost for local graffiti. These days, the signs of the times are "I❤Ron," "Latin Raza

Chicano," and "R-Man is Rough."

The fence has been forced open below street level. A well-trod path cuts down the bank, through the brush and across three sets of train tracks to an opening on the other side. At mid-morning, I watch a young man holding a bouquet of leaves saunter across the tracks. 15 seconds later a girl takes the same route. 15 seconds after her, the 10:05 out of Vendome Station barrels through. Plug up this hole and there are a dozen more just as useful.

Between Cavendish Boulevard and the Loyola playing field, the track's embankment rises above the street. It's easy to walk over the poorly maintained fence. This is Canadian Pacific property. It's private land, but there are few legible signs warning errant dog walkers or flower pickers off. Once here, however, it's the signs of the wild that require attention. Skunks lie in culverts. Poison ivy grows green and scarlet. Brambles tear at clothing. Vines run amuck with tendrils that climb to the tops of telephone poles. In several places, the plants weave a heavy carpet through the long fence and bend it to the ground.

Fortunately, there is enough to harvest along the fence without venturing in. This week the schach cutters were out. Schach, which rhymes with Bach, is the boughs and grasses that cover huts built for the Jewish festival of Sukot. During biblical times, these were set up for farmers who stayed in their fields throughout the harvest. Sukot is often celebrated the around same time as Canadian Thanksgiving.

There's a lot of schach to be had along the tracks. It's been a good harvest for everyone.

TEL-AIDE

Behind the door of room 126, the city throbs with pain. The door is ordinary and anonymous. There's no sign indicating what goes on inside every hour of the day, every day of the year. It's a plain green door, at the end of a nondescript corridor, in an undistinguished downtown building.

Room 126 has a small bank of telephones. They ring constantly. Last Monday night four people were answering them. They sat in small, semi-enclosed cubicles, their eyes were focused on someone beyond this room, on something else, taking the next call, making contact. The conversations began in similar patterns: " Hi... yeah... I'm o.k. how are you?... what's the matter?... yeah... what's going on?... ok... just relax a bit... we'll talk..."

There's no call waiting here, no call forwarding, no ident-a-call or call display. No phone numbers are mentioned. No names are known. "Hi ... no we don't give our names and we don't need to know yours...You want, you can call me John. No, that's not my real name; but you can call me John... what do you want to talk about?..."

This is Montreal's Tel-Aide service. It's based on an unspoken bond. You call and I will listen. You call and you won't get a list of numbers to punch your way through. You call and you won't get an answering service. You call and I'll be here.

It's hard work. You need to be an active listener. Sometimes volunteers forget what to say, sometimes they forget how to listen. There are two lists by each telephone. One has suggestions on how to keep involved while staying detached. It says "Some active listening reminders: Paraphrase, Empathy, Attentive, Avoid one upmanship, Be non-judgmental, Validate feelings, Avoid talking about yourself, Don't give advice, Respect for oneself, Respect caller's reality."

If we all had this list near our phones, the world would be a better place.

The other list is an index to urban pain. It's a glossary to help volunteers track what callers describe: basic needs, loneliness, depression, illness, relationships, work/studies, pregnancy/abortion, sexuality, suicide, violence.

Most calls last from 5 to 15 minutes. Listeners make notes when the call is over. As the evening progresses, their logs fill up: "angry about...," "depressed about ...," "teenager thrown out of house...," "feeling like an outsider," "just needing to talk to someone, on welfare," "father abused her, wants a family." No names, just despair from a lonely city in the night.

Sometimes there's a call, a few words and a lot of heavy breathing. The volunteer breaks the caller's rhythm "yeah...say, are you masturbating?... Why don't you call back when you're finished?" In less than ten seconds, the phone rings. "Hi... you're finished? ... let's talk."

Sometimes there's a wail. The call is private but you can hear a scream across the room. There's muffled crying and the listener patiently talks someone through something. This call lasts almost an hour. Suddenly the volunteer writes down a phone number. She calls 911. It's a suicide. He cut his wrists before he called Tel-Aide but wouldn't give his number until the end. Maybe it wasn't too deep, maybe he wanted help after all. A couple of times a month this happens.

Listeners get extensive training before they become Tel-Aide volunteers. Each promises to spend at least one evening every two weeks in this room for a year. There's a coffee machine and comfortable chairs to help them through their shifts.

Then there are the notes tacked up near the water cooler. "A caller said to say a heart-felt thank you to the listener who helped him on …" " … veut remercier une bénévole pour son aide lors de sa tentative de suicide il y a une semaine," "… remercie de lui qui a sauvé la vie, intoxiqué jeudi soir."

It's late in the evening outside room 126. There are fewer lights on in the apartments nearby. Downtown traffic is sparse and the loudest noise comes from the occasional bus rumbling by.

Inside, there's a constancy of hushed refrains. It's like slow jazz with endless variations on a few basic themes: "Hi…what happened?… how are you now?… You feel that everything went wrong today?… Let's talk about you, not your brother's girl friend… That's tough talk. Are you tough?… What do you think it will take to make you feel happy?… Good luck… OK… Have a good night… we'll talk again sometime."

VIOLENCE

It happened a couple of nights ago. Louise was in bed, asleep. At 1:15 in the morning she heard a window smash "like Arnold Schwarzenegger coming through with his fists." She had a phone by the bed and dialed 911. The police were at her door in three minutes and a second squad car a minute or so later. It was the wind unseating a poorly fitted window at the top of her back door.

Louise lives alone, a few houses up the street from us. She says that she hesitated before calling the police. "I don't want to be seen as one of those spinsters who call every time there is a creak in the floor."

After the cops left she sat up for hours, calling friends and making a mental list of the violence she has seen or experienced.

Here's the list: At 13, Lousie and her friend hitched a ride and two drunk guys tried to molest them. Once her mother was held as a hostage at gunpoint by a robber. At 25 Louise was raped. A few years ago, there was a shooting on our street. Last year, she was caught in a riot the last Carifest parade.

The horror is not that this happened, but that so little of it seems exceptional. Similar stories to hers have happened to people in my family.

Several times in the past few years Louise has seen people walking through neighbourhood backyards at 3 or 4 in the morning. Once she called a neighbour and the two of them went out with crowbars and chased the men away. "I'm not going to do that now," she says. "I'll call the police."

For Louise, it was the smashed window that escalated the violence across the line. Not the window itself but, as she puts it, "the immediate assumption of danger, the fear of that danger and the subsequent mental list of past danger that put me over the top."

"I've had it," she told me. "I give up. I want some measure of security in my own house. I want to feel that I can keep them out for ever. I don't want to be killed."

Charts are good at showing the crime "out there," but they can't define the boundry that each of us may have to cross. That is a line I can't define, but I know that I crossed it when I started making sure my mother was safely in her car, with the engine running, before I let her out of my sight, or when I began driving our dinner guests to the Métro station at night rather than letting them walk. Somewhere, I crossed the line when I decided to take a longer walk home along brightly lit streets, in the evening, rather than a shorter one through an industrial part of town.

I'm not too sure if Montreal is changing or if it is me. At 20 I walked anywhere and felt invulnerable. Now I'm much less sure. Like Louise, I walk quickly at night, my keys are at hand, and I don't make eye contact.

Last summer Louise put bars on her back windows. This year she plans to put them on the front and make the back door more secure. "I don't feel imprisoned," she says. "I believe that I'm keeping the nuts out. Violence is a fact of life."

ZEN

It was Tuesday, so Masaê Nakauchi and Sonya Williams were talking to each other in English. Nakauchi and Williams work at the Japanese pavilion at the Botanical Gardens. They work different shifts. On the days their schedules overlap, they spend some time improving their linguistic proficiency. On Tuesdays they speak to each other in English. On Wednesdays, it's Japanese; and on Thursdays, it's French. Now there's a refreshing approach.

I had come to the garden to soothe a referendum damaged spirit. The caustic acid applied to our collective souls by our premier's concession speech still hurt. Meeting Williams and Nakauchi made me feel a little better.

The Japanese garden has been open since 1988. It's a series of small gardens and ponds that surround a larger pavilion and art gallery. In warmer weather there is an outstanding collection of bonsai outdoors, and large multi-coloured carp swim in pools. There are huts in the gardens. It's a nice place to rest and contemplate the carp, life, or whatever you want.

There's no TV here, no newspapers, just a soft gurgle from a small fountain and the call from an occasional bird as it flies through. Inside the pavilion are muted tones of traditional Japanese music.

The pavilion is built around a classic Zen garden. This one is modeled on a temple in Kyoto. It's inordinately simple, just 11 stones of different sizes in a sea of well-raked gravel. The garden has no focal point. The stones are arranged so that there is no center in the sense that many North American or European gardens have one.

The space is formless. It forces the viewer into a more restful way of thinking, looking at the rocks and imagining them as mountains rising above a sea of crushed stones that has been raked into patterns of clouds or eddies or waves. After a week of political turmoil, it seemed a good place to find a little calm and serenity.

The guardian of the garden is, surprisingly, not Japanese. Raking gravel is hard work, traditionally done by Zen monks or, as happens in Montreal, by strong Caucasians keen on tending it. This fall it's been under Williams' care. She's a tall, multilingual Australian who came to Canada on a work permit.

Williams recently finished a Commerce degree. She says this is a typical Australian thing to do "one year on, one year off." So far she has spent a year each in Belgium and Japan. She taught English in a school near Tokyo and was surprised that almost all the teachers had been recruited from McGill. So Canada became the next stop on her world tour. She came over in September, walked into the garden as a visitor, surprised the staff by speaking fluent Japanese, and was offered a job as a guide.

It's hard work to rake the garden. This is gravel, not grass. The rake handle is steel and weighs several kilograms. The tines are thick, v-shaped, and made of wood. Leaves blow over the walls and are gathered by hand. It takes Williams two hours to clean the garden. Then she rakes the gravel into it's distinctive whorls, waves, and lines.

The Zen garden has a remarkable effect on people. It is art, but one in which the artist says as little as possible. Viewers bring their interpretations and each is correct. In a week of absolutes, where the fate of our country hinged on fractions, it is refreshing to be somewhere where all you have to do is let your mind wander and relax.

As Williams and I looked into the garden, a large tour group entered one end of the pavilion. You could hear their chatter down the hall. When the group walked in front of the garden, everyone stopped talking. Williams said that always happens. She said that people from Japan sometimes kneel and pray.

Towards the end of my visit, I noticed a man and woman sitting in front of the garden but not paying attention to it. They were an older couple who could have been characters from a Michel Tremblay play. It was the day after the referendum but they weren't talking about politics. They were talking about bingo. It seemed that there was a particularly good place that they wanted to go to near the Henri-Bourassa metro station. Suddenly the wife pointed to the garden and said "look, look at the mountain out there." For a long while they sat silently, the bingo forgotten, both looking at a quiet country that each may have been discovering for the first time.

—~—

3 STARS

It's easy to miss the 3 Stars resto bar on Victoria Ave. It's sandwiched between Ghetto Style Accessories and the Duc Thanh grocery store. The sign is small, just three stars, one for each of the original partners.

The 3 Stars isn't going to take away customers from the Ritz. There's a half-dozen tables, a pool game, and a bank of video lotteries against the wall. Most nights, the menu is simple: vegetable or meat curry. For an appetizer, there's dahl vadei, a spicy fritter. One bite demands a drink. Whiskey is cheap at the 3 Stars. Beer is cheaper.

"It's like a fast food men's club," says Ratnam Siva, one of the owners. He came to Montreal in 1984, a refugee from Sri Lanka. Almost everyone at the 3 Stars is a refugee from Sri Lanka.

A few years back, this place was Mexican. It folded because there's not much of a Mexican community here. Then it was either Spanish or Somali. No one at the 3 Stars is sure which, but it didn't last long. Last year Govenda Palli Chandran, Siva, and another friend started paying rent.

Siva and Chandran worked in factories and restaurants before they opened up the 3 Stars. Siva isn't happy about being a boss. He hates the paperwork. He opens at 11 am and takes a break in the evening when Chandran comes in. He comes back if it's busy and sometimes locks up at 3 in the morning. The third partner couldn't take it and left six months ago.

Chandran is making kottu roti in the back. This is the 3 Stars nightly dish. He chops a pile of onions and fills a colander with thinly sliced leeks. He stirs containers of mutton and beef, the two choices for meat curry. Then he waits. Every order is made fresh.

At one table, men snack from a bowl of marinated fish they've brought into the restaurant. They share a piece with the owners. "Sri Lankan fish?" I ask. "No," says one, "Canadian fish, Sri Lankan recipe."

Chandran moves to the grill and starts cooking. The vegetables hit the oil and sizzle. He adds fresh green chilis, spices, the meat curry and bits of chopped bread called roti. He cuts into the mound, mixing and tossing, as the steam rises in front of him.

Chandran came in 1986. His sister was here before him. A few years later, he brought over his mother and brother.

Next to the bar, a white guy who looks like he slept in a ditch, is playing the video slots. He smokes heavily and ignores the message that occasionally flashes across the screen, "in moderation, a game remains a game." The guy asks for $25 worth of loonies. He goes through them and gets the same again. After about an hour, the machine spits out a piece of paper. He's won $125.

In 1988, $125 was the fee Chandran paid to the government of Canada to bring his mother over. This year, we raised the ante. Now newcomers must pay $1500 for each family member they bring here. That's a lot of kottu roti.

A few months ago, Chandran's sister opened a fast food restaurant in Toronto. His brother has a small catering company. Between them they have created another half dozen jobs.

An Indian video plays over the bar. Boy meets girl, boy loses girl, boy sings lament. A few regulars communally drain a litre of whiskey. Later they may play cards.

One man at the table was accepted as a refugee three years ago. He's still waiting for the papers he needs to bring his family over. He can work here. He can live here. But until he can bring his family here, it's not much of a life. In the mean time, he waits at the 3 Stars.

ALL THE RIGHT MOVES

Burky Reid's got all the right moves for a point guard. He holds back and takes in the play. Then he gets the ball and feints to the right. He shoots out an arm and scrambles low. He moves around men twice his size. He dribbles twice, finds a piece of air and squeezes off a two point jump shot.

This is the NDG Black Community Association Summer Basketball League. Most players are in college or working. Most are over 6 feet tall. A couple are big enough to be line backers for the Als.

Burky is 17 years old and 5'4." He's going into his last year at Mount Royal High. Last year he played with 4 basketball teams. Two weeks ago he scored 22 points.

This week isn't good. His right knee hurts. "Jumper's knee," he says, "Everyone gets it." He's cautious. He plans to be in the Martin Luther King tournament this weekend. He'll be up against players his age from Boston, New York City and Toronto. Last year his team won their division.

This is a serious tournament. Scouts show up from American universities. Even a 5'4" point guard who scrambles like a spider has a chance for glory.

But tonight it's the NDG Summer League and Burky's team wins the first match. We watch another game together. It's a bust. At the end of the first half, Team 6 has scored only 19 points. The Enterprise has 42. The coach of The Enterprise, Stan

Williams, tells me that several of his players are up from US colleges. William's team looks impressive until Burky tells me it's third in the league.

The last game of the night features the league's two best teams. Burky says to watch for number 4 in the blue jersey. It's Trevor Williams. Point guard. "He was once my size," says Burky. Williams is now 6 feet tall. He's 30 years old and a former member of Canada's national team.

At times, when he takes the ball, Williams can hold back time. Tonight he watches, watches, and positions his team mates. It takes a moment. It takes an eternity. Then he lets the ball loose and the game erupts. At the sidelines, Burky is motionless. He has stopped rubbing his leg. His eyes follow Williams. The youth studies the general commanding his troops.

Later I ask Williams about Burky. He says the kid has tremendous potential. "But he has to learn that basketball isn't just physical. It's a mental game. That's what I want him to learn."

Williams has a couple of small businesses in Little Burgundy, including a summer basketball camp. The picture on the camp's brochure shows Williams dribbling past Magic Johnson when Canada played the US dream team in the Olympics.

Williams' basketball camp has grown from 18 kids, 4 years ago to 300 now. The cost is $75 a week, but it's only open for 4 weeks. The camp brochure sports a Reebok logo and gives promotional credit to Nettoyeur Boulay and a couple of local sport shops. There's no mention of government funding. Williams says he gets only a few hundred dollars from municipal, provincial or federal governments.

Williams' partner, Dean Smith, has another perspective. He says that it costs $65,000 to keep a kid in a youth detention centre for a year. He says with much less than that, they'd have the camp open all summer. There would be that much more opportunity to keep kids off the streets and out of trouble.

Smith and Williams have been watching Burky. He'll go to the camp this summer, maybe be a counsellor next year. "Without basketball, he'd be selling crack," says Smith. "I should know. I've got plenty of friends who are now in prison."

COLONIAL BATH

The boys don't come on Tuesdays to the Colonial Steam Baths. Tuesday is ladies day, so the boys don't come. The boys come on Wednesday, sometimes Thursday, often Sunday.

The boys are Herbie and Alvin and Arthur "the butcher" and Jack who just opened up a new clothing store on St. Denis St. and Bob who used to teach at Concordia and Hymie who used to be in the fruit business and Vic who works out at Le Sanctuaire six mornings a week and his cousin Charlie.

"Always call him Mr. Steinberg," says Vic of his cousin. Mr. Steinberg is 79. He's the oldest of the boys.

"I've been coming here 50 years," says Jack. "I've been coming here since I was 4," says Charlie. "My father came here," says Alvin. "He didn't have a bath at home."

There are two steam rooms at the Colonial. The wet steam comes from pipes. The dry steam has a furnace filled with rocks lugged from the river. "River rocks hold the water better," says Hymie.

The boys are getting the dry steam room ready. Hymie lays out the towels and buckets of cold water. Vic opens the furnace door. "Watch what you're doing," says Charlie. "Don't pour too much water on it." "I'll do it my way," says Vic. "Cover your ears." The steam bellows out with enough force to make them pop.

The boys climb onto benches that rise against two walls of the room. The higher the climb, the greater the heat. Arthur lies down and Charlie takes a heavy scrub brush from a soap filled bucket. The brush is made from hundreds of maple leaves, their stems bound around a thick staff. The soap has softened the leaves to the texture of silk. The boys slowly brush each other down with a soapy pummel.

The leaves are thick and loamy. When they move off the body, steam sears the skin. The person getting scrubbed has a cold wet towel over his head. Everyone else is naked, except for hats.

The hats are felt. "The same material as a fedora," says Hymie. They're dunked in cold water. The body can take a lot more heat if the head thinks it's cool.

The boys leave the dry steam. "Take a cold shower," says Charlie. The water pours over me like mercy. "Turn around and put your hands against the wall," says Charlie. He starts to pound backs as if nothing else could get the circulation going.

Hymie brings fresh towels for the wet steam. This is the hot one. Ian MacDonald comes in. Ian is 6'8", a former Alouette, now an actor and stunt man. He bends to keep his face out of the highest steam. "Some of these guys are too macho," he says.

Charlie gives another rub down. Vic goes upstairs to get food ready. "You like matjes herring?" asks Arthur. I ask him if it's from Snowdon Delicatessen. "Hey Charlie," he yells, ""the kid wants to know if I get the herring from Snowdon. Hah! I buy wholesale."

Upstairs, a couple of the boys are draped with sheets, taking naps. "Have a drink," says Arthur.

There's a bottle of Smirnoff, another of Tanguernay, some tonic water, and a can of tomato juice. The boys gather around the table. "I'm not talking to Jack," says Arthur, "just one of those things. Don't worry, some day we'll talk."

Vic brings out the food: thickly cut tomatoes, sweet bermuda onions, chopped egg, lettuce, cucumber, pumpernickle, pickles, bowls of fruit and a fresh pineapple. "You know how Hymie picks a pineapple?" Vic laughs, "He finds an Italian." "This isn't much," Bob apologies. "Usually there's smoked meat or a chicken."

It's almost six o'clock. The boys have to leave early. They're off to see Jack's new store. Arthur has a suggestion. "Hey," he says, "I got a headline for you. Dirty old men become clean old men at the shvitz."

GRAFFITI

It's late Saturday afternoon and Montreal's top graffiti artists are putting signatures to their latest pieces in a new show.

"We're not artists," Seaz shouts over the hip hop music bouncing off the walls. "I'm a writer. If I was an artist, I'd be accepted."

Seaz is in his mid-twenties. He works in an arcade. Before that he was a security guard. He said that he spends about $200 a week on paints. The multi-coloured piece he was doing, consisting only of his name, would use about 10 or 11 cans at $6.00 a pop.

There's no Canada Council grants out there to help them. For the most part, there are cops and quick escapes and a wild free flowing signature for the rest of the world to decipher.

Once you know the names, the tags, their pieces are easier to follow. There's Flow, Kid Search, Timer, Seaz and a half dozen others working here. Their pieces cover several interior walls in a converted mattress factory beside the Lachine canal.

This graffiti jam is a show where writers go legit and if a movement goes legit, it needs someone to legitimize it. Enter sociologist and art historian, Louise Gauthier. She's doing her PhD thesis on graffiti.

Gauthier printed a one-page guide to the show, called Aerosol Funk. "Watch for the skillful manipulation of the can of aerosol paint," she wrote, "the exuberant colour combinations, the symbols used and the characters depicted, the blunt lettering, and the chaotic spatial compositions including the 3-D pull effect."

"Look," she commands "these are very personal renderings."

Gauthier's thesis advisor said that Montreal graffiti is different from the work in New York or other large American cities. "It's tamer, not as violent," he told her.

By late afternoon, the gallery air is thick with aerosol fumes. Fans are blowing, windows are open and most of the writers wear masks. Several writers have detailed drawings in front of them. The more wild the tags, the more work goes into them.

Flow is an acclaimed writer. If you've seen his name, you've seen his work. It's on freight cars, tunnels, and public places. He works three or four hours on a piece, usually at night. This is one of the first times he's worked inside.

"It's nice to relax instead of looking over your shoulder," he says, "but I'd rather be painting outside." Would he only paint legally if he could? "No, I'd do both. I like the adrenalin, the rush. I don't drink, I don't do drugs. My drug is painting. That's where I spend my money."

"It's not just vandalism," adds Seaz. "It's an art form. It's part of a culture that includes hip hop and fashion and skate boards. We have rules. We don't trash cars or churches or private property. I do it for the fame. This gets me around."

JOHNNY CHIN

Johnny Chin is never where you expect him. Ask his customers. They never know where he'll make his next batch of candy. Ask his in-laws. They're going to be surprised if he moves back to Hong Kong, when everyone else seems to be leaving.

You know Johnny if you've seen a man in Chinatown stretching corn syrup into gossamer. He always starts his spiel the same way.

"This is regular corn syrup," he says holding up a half-cup glob. "Just like you put on pancakes, but firmer." He pulls it into a circle. "Now we have a chinese Dunkin' Donut," he says and dunks it into corn starch. He doubles the donut on itself, pulls, and shows four strands where there were two. He doubles it again and there are eight. "I'm from King Kong," he tells the dozen or so people watching him. "That's near Hong Kong." A family from Chicoutimi laughs. A couple from the Lion's convention looks confused.

The patter continues in French, English and only he knows which Chinese dialects. On most nights he can separate that half cup of jellied corn syrup 12 times. That's 4096 strands, each as thin as spider's thread. It's hard to tell which the crowd finds more impressive: Johnny's skill or a practical application of logarithms.

He lays an outstretched arm's worth of webbing

across a table and pinches off a couple of inches. He spreads some crushed peanuts, sesame seeds and chocolate on the strands and folds them into a nugget as thick as a thumb.

The candies sell for 50 cents each. That's not bad for a few cents worth of corn syrup and crushed nuts. By day, Johnny's an accountant. At night and on holidays, he demonstrates "the secret art of the emperor's Dragon's Beard Candy."

Johnny doesn't advertise his locations. The city doesn't give permits to street entertainers who work with food.

Johnny's wife shows up to help him pack. He introduces her as Pauline. She came to Canada four months ago. I've known Johnny for years and never knew he was married.

"My first marriage was 18 years ago," he says. "I married a Quebecoise. I was attracted to the exotic. The marriage didn't work out. "We had a son. He's sixteen and lives with me."

A few years ago, Johnny returned to visit his family in Hong Kong. A friend of a friend arranged for him to meet some women in a small town west of Canton. The meetings started at six-thirty one evening with a different match every half-hour through the night. Pauline was walking across the street when he saw her.

"I knew I wanted a country girl," Johnny says. "My family thought I was crazy. 'First you marry a Quebecer, then you marry a girl from Communist China. What's wrong with someone from Hong Kong?' I told them they don't know what I need. Those women from Hong Kong want too much."

I asked Johnny if his in-laws know what he does in Montreal. "They never asked," he said. "It was very relaxed. Pauline's family didn't care what kind of car I drove or what I did for a living."

A friend drives a van onto the sidewalk. Johnny folds up the table. Pauline takes care of the containers. They're packed in less than a minute. It's a routine that Johnny's perfected through six summers on the streets of Montreal.

"This could be my last year," he says. "My parents are in their seventies. I've been away 21 years. It's time to go back. Time to do my duty as a son."

I ask how Pauline will like going back. "Her parents will wonder why she was away only one year," Johnny says. "But I think there will be lots of opportunity in Hong Kong. You have to a have a different point of view to get ahead."

KASH THE BAGEL BAKER

I went to see a man about a bagel. This isn't as odd as it may seem. If there's one food that has become the essence of la grande bouffe that is Montreal, it is the bagel.

I once had hopes for the crêpe. There was a time when you could get great crêpes in almost any part of town. Forget doughy restaurant pancakes. A good crêpe is the colour of burnt gold, as thin as parchment. It covers a dinner plate. The filling satiates the soul: ice cream and apples, or cheese with ham, or fresh asparagus and hollandaise.

Crêpes symbolized what Montreal offered North America: great taste with European finesse. Crêpes defined us as culinary hedonists. They showed how different we were from our large neighbour to the south whose gastronomic identity was fixed on the mass produced, uniformly grey hamburger.

A few crêperies remain, but for the most part, the crêpe proved to be a fad. Louis Tavan owned several in his La Crêpe Bretonne chain in the 1970s. At one time, Tavan had almost half the restaurants on Mountain street. They all disappeared when his company folded.

Similarly, I have, at various times, put my faith in un steamé all dressed, smoked meat, and even poutine. But the number of hot dog and smoked meat stands are declining and french fries covered with gravy and melted cheese curds remain an eccentric attraction at best.

Surprisingly, it is the Montreal bagel which has the best chance of defining the city's culinary character. It is available everywhere. It appears hard to penetrate but quickly yields under pressure. It began as two distinct varieties: poppy seed or sesame.

The Montreal bagel differs from the New York or Toronto version. The New York bagel is called a water bagel. It is chewier and not as crisp. Unlike the Montreal bagel, the dough is made without eggs. The New York bagel tastes best with robustly flavored cream cheeses.

The Toronto bagel is usually made in a gas oven. It is not burnished by the scorching wood-fired heat from which a true Montreal bagel emerges. The Montreal bagel is great by itself. The Toronto one is excellent for dunking in coffee.

"Bagel" comes from the Yiddish beygel via the German words "beugel" meaning a round loaf of bread and "bügel," a ring. Until the 1970s, it was an exotic Jewish bread. You had to drive to St. Viateur street to get the authentic version. Now, they're as common as croissants.

There is a new bagel cafe serving espresso and wood-fired bagels on the trendiest section of Mount Royal east. There are wood fired bagel bakeries in Le Faubourg and Plaza Côte-des-Neiges. At one supermarket in Saint Laurent, the bagel bakers speak Spanish. At D.A.D.'s bagels, the common language is Punjabi.

The city's oldest ovens are at the Fairmount Bagel bakery and the St. Viateur Bagel Shop. Once, the original owners were partners. They were Jews from eastern European families. They sold bagels from a pushcart near Schwartz's on the Main.

One bagel lover recently boasted that his bagel baker was so authentic, he wore a Jewish skullcap. The man I went to see about a bagel also wears a head covering. It's a turban. Kash is a Sikh. He says he began baking bagels because "some of my best friends were Jewish." He thought it would be a good business.

Kash spent many years in the Indian army. He always imagined himself as a leader of men. Today he gets to his store at 6 in the morning. He works 12 hour days. He stokes his oven with hard wood and sells Roumanian sausage, coffee, cheese knishes, and smoked salmon to go with his bagels. He also sells baguettes, empanadas, samosas and tzaziki. Kash speaks 5 languages. Yiddish is not one of them.

The key to a Montreal bagel is it's temperament. It must be coddled in sweet, hot water and tempered in fire. It retains a crunch at the first bite and a malty flavor within. It freezes well and reheats beautifully in a toaster oven.

Bagel dough is softer than most bread doughs. One of the first dishes my daughter tried to make was bagels. We made them out of left over pizza dough. Rolling out the dough into snakes and then joining the ends together is child's play. The technique is more important than the details of a recipe.

If you want an authentic Montreal bagel recipe, however, it's helpful to know a master baker. Step this way Marcy Goldman. She offers a recipe from her new book "A Treasury of Jewish Holiday Baking" published by Doubleday (1998). Marcy is one of the best bakers in the country. You can reach her at www.betterbaking.com.

Bagels

1 3/4 cups water
1/2 ounce fresh yeast
or 2 1/2 teaspoons dry yeast*
 pinch of sugar
3 tablespoons oil
2 tablespoons beaten egg
1 tablespoon malt powder *
1 1/2 teaspoons salt, optional
5 tablespoons sugar
4 1/2 - 5 cups bread flour

* Marcy likes Fermipan dry yeast for bagels. Malt powder is usually available at health food stores.

Kettle water:
6 quarts water
1/3 cup honey

Garnish:
1 1/2 cups sesame seed or poppy seeds
      (or half and half)

Stir the water, yeast, and pinch of sugar together. Let this stand a couple of minutes, allowing the yeast to swell or dissolve.

Whisk in the sugar, beaten egg, vegetable oil, and malt. Fold in most of the flour. (If using fresh yeast, crumble it into warm water along with a pinch of sugar. Let it stand a couple of minutes and then add the other ingredients as you would for the dry yeast method).

Knead this for 10-12 minutes to form a stiff, smooth dough, adding additional flour as required.

Cover the dough with a tea towel or inverted bowl and let it rest ten minutes.

Take out three large cookie or baking sheets. Line one with a kitchen towel and another with baking parchment.

Fill a large soup pot or Dutch oven three quarters full with water. Add honey and salt. Bring the water to a boil.

Meanwhile, divide the dough into 12 sections and form these into 10 inch strips. Form each strip into a bagel ring. Place them on a third cookie sheet. Let the dough rise 12-16 minutes until bagels are slightly puffed up.

Preheat the oven to 450° F.

Boil the bagels 1 1/2 minutes each, turning them over once in the process.

Place them on the towel lined sheet to drain them. Then sprinkle each generously with sesame or poppy seeds. (Montreal Bagels are more seeded than bagels made elsewhere).

Place them on the parchment lined sheet.

Put the baking sheet in the oven, reduce the heat to 425° F. Bake the bagels about 15-22 minutes, or until they are a dark golden brown. Turn them over once when they are just about done.

KAHNAWAKE

Mike Rice and Josie Curotte are driving through Kahnawake, population about 8000, unemployment over 50%. I see rural poverty. Mike sees entrepreneurs.

The car is a big old Ford that's soft as a pillow over the ruts and smells like it has a gas leak.

Josie drives. Mike talks. He points to where light industry could be set up. We drive past an unmanned security shack with an upside down stop sign. We're in Kahnawake village now. The police cars have a Mohawk's profile on their doors.

Josie drives past a couple of houses with signs for cheap cigars and cigarettes at $2 a pack. Mike ignores them. That's not the kind of entrepreneurship he has in mind.

Mike and Josie want to show us another side of Kahnawake. They've organized the Walking Heritage Tour. A Belgian tourist says that Montreal friends warned her white women are killed on the reservation. Mike and Josie say nothing. They've heard as much before and worse.

Mike is 27. Last fall, he graduated from McGill. During his first two years at university, he lived in Montreal with Chinese friends and worked in their family business. He made tofu to help pay his tuition. Mike writes for the weekly newspaper Eastern Door and announces lacrosse games on the local radio station. He canoes 10 km. a day.

Josie has a degree in anthropology and works as a judge with the local court. She's in her 40s and a grandmother. She's just come back from a week at a Laurentian camp teaching people how to do native beadwork.

"You've only got a couple of choices here," Mike says. "You can blame your problem on the outside or you can try and do something about it."

A tourist bus pulls up for mass at St. Francis-Xavier church, the shrine of Kateri Tekakwitha. Josie tells our group that Kateri is "one miracle away from sainthood." She says that not everyone sees this is a positive role model. "In our culture we revere women who support the family. Of course the priest will tell you a different story."

Josie and Mike don't give the traditional tour. It doesn't include "Kahnawake's Old Indian Village Featuring Keepers of the Eastern Door Mohawk Singers and Dancers. Gates Open 12 noon, Showtime: 1 p.m. & 3.p.m."

Their tour is a trudge through history. We discuss the past. We look at magnificent thick-walled 17th century houses on River Rd. Some owners restored their buildings; others tore them down. "Not everyone respects what the French brought here," says Mike.

We end up at the new wooden Longhouse. It's a traditionalist meeting hall. Not everyone feels comfortable in the Longhouse. Then again, not everyone feels comfortable at St. Francis-Xavier.

For a long time, Mohawks had their own nation. In 1876, Canada imposed the Indian Act. It tried to suppress traditional beliefs and accelerate native assimilation into European culture. Only recently, have our first nations started redefining what their independence means within Canada.

Mike and Josie say they don't see themselves as Canadians or Americans. They talk about how the government carved away Kahnawake's best farm land for the seaway in the 1950s, how their parents had to have travel papers to leave their community, how those who left for higher education lost their status as natives, and how those on reservations couldn't vote in federal elections until the 1960s. "A lot of Jews tell us it was once something like this for them," Josie says.

At the Cultural Center, one wall shows seven generations of families. "Our culture believes that you may live to see the sixth generation but you always have to plan for the seventh, the one you'll never see," Josie says, "you have to anticipate the impact you are going to have." She pauses. "The Indian Act was created about seven generations ago. We're just starting to see the impact now."

NEW YEAR'S WITH THE DOCTOR

Long brown fingers prod the keyboard. They graze a row of buttons and press "style select." They move up to the next row to number 45 "twist." The beat comes out boom ta da boom ta da boom.

"I'm Douglas Rodrigues but you can call me the doctor." A voice like a shovel full of gravel hits the mike and cuts through the crowd. "Mes amis, la vie est très belle. Un jour à la fois. Let's twist again, like we did at the Esquire Show Bar."

What club are you going to tonight? The doctor's working. What club did your parents go to on New Year's Eve: Butch Bouchard's, Cleopatra, Casa Loma, Rockhead's Paradise, The Rainbow, Champs, Joe Louis' hotel in Harlem? He's been there.

"God took away, but he gave me more than he took," the doctor says. "I was born blind. I left Puerto Rico in 1939 . All the handicapped kids were transferred to the States at the beginning of the war. They sent me to Batavia New York, to the biggest blind school in the world. I didn't see my folks for 5 years. God gave me the music. Blind people used to cane chairs. I learned classical. I played boogie woogie and they rapped my hands. No one would pay minorities to play classical."

The beat changes and he plays a merengue. People get up to dance. He swings into Santa Claus is Coming to Town and cuts to Five Foot Two. Quick fingers, simple chords.

The doctor is 6'3'' and gaunt. "I lost my wife two years ago. My weight has dropped from 227 to 190." He takes a break and someone brings over food. He eats a couple of sandwiches, a plate of maccaroni salad and vegetables. Someone hands him some cake. He keeps his plate raised until he has three pieces. "Je mange comme un cochon. After my wife died I didn't do anything. Then God kicked me in the ass and said get out and I was playing again.

"I play four or five times a week. Yesterday I had two gigs. I got to sleep at 2 and I was up at 10. I get phone calls at night. A lot of people talk to me. There's so many people alone. One woman, her boyfriend died right in her arms. I just talked to to her. You got to like yourself. You got to say I can do it. I got a girl friend now. Her name is Cecile. A friend of mine is 60. He got a young girl pregrant, 28. That thing between your legs can get you into trouble."

The voice grates into New York, New York. The doctor stops singing but the hands continue. All of a sudden a real jazz riff rips from the keyboard. No beat box, no supporting medley. An old coin from long ago drops and the doctor takes us back to Louis Armstrong playing the Fox Theatre in Detroit, back to combos, stride piano, and big bands. Then he swings into B.B. King and brings it home.

These days the doctor's clubs are the Royal Vic, the Julius Richardson. Tonight he's playing the Good Shepherd. "I don't do Guns & Roses. I do the Beatles, Fats Domino. The only rap I do is Christmas presents. I still got to pay my rent, telephone, electricity. I play for Seniors. Seniors don't have Musique Plus."

The wallabees stick to the beat and red sox dart

from under the cuffs. The rhythm changes to a polka, then slows for O Bon Sapin. He opens the crystal on his Seiko and touches the hands. The music stops. A woman brings over a cup of tea. "Put some sugar in it," he says, "put a smile in it."

—~ —

SEPARATIST TANGO

Pierre Monette moves like the tango. Just when you think you've got him, he slips somewhere else. Slow, Slow, quick, quick, quick, hold.

Call him a nationalist. He says he's an independentist. What's the difference? "Nationalists are narrow minded, they are open to fascist thinking. My dream is for a separate Quebec but one that is open to all cultures... We had one real referendum. That was in 1980. Now referendums are part of our folklore. We have learned that solutions can never be found through politics. Solutions will be found at Schwartz's."

He offers angst for most of the other independentists. "I could even imagine that a hundred years from now, no one will speak French; but that will be ok as long as we have developed a distinct culture." Slow, slow, quick, quick, quick.

For some, this is heresy. Monette is a tenured teacher of French at the CEGEP du Vieux Montreal. "My students are the future of Quebec but we are creating a generation of utilitarians. They know how to write but they never speak of fiction or style. They know that poetry may rhyme and that's it."

Monette is known for books on the tango and a long essay, "L'immigrant Montréal," that argues for a more open society. His latest book is going to offend a lot of people.

This one's called "Pour en finir avec les inté-

gristes" – Let's stop the fundamentalists. It's a dia-
tribe against the politically correct, against politi-
cans and writers who promote "a certain kind of
culture." Our goal should not be "to assimilate others," he says, "but to create something together."
Slow, slow, quick, quick, quick.

Monette speaks English. He teaches French. He
is a third generation Italian. He is totally Québecois
and a constant paradox. Bill 101 is necessary, "it's
part of the French tradition to protect language."
Then he shows that the French language is in no
danger of fading. He provides pages of statistics to
prove how French Montreal has become.

Monette went to Argentina to research "Le
guide du Tango." He came back with a vision of
what Quebec could become: a place where people
from all cultures bring something new and share a
common language. "Argentina came into its own in
this century. It was transformed by immigration,"
he says. "Today there is one Argentine de souche for
every 3 immigrants."

This is a man who loves to play with ideas, but
he's never been to Toronto, the Rockies or any part
of Canada outside Quebec. "If I go, there will
always be a little voice in my head. It will say this
country is supposed to be open to me, it is supposed to be bilingual, but it's not. It's not my country. I don't want to hear that voice." To talk with
Monette is to dance the dialectic. Just when you
think you are leading, he turns.

I left Monette's flat and walked to the
Sherbrooke Metro. In minutes, I entered the
Montreal Monette may have in mind. First I heard
the music. Jacques Phénix, a Québecois who had
studied in India, was playing a raga on a sitar. While
he played, I chatted with Yvon Ganneville, a man

who used to wander the streets. He looked clean and well. He was making a little money selling copies of L'itinéraire, a magazine put out by the homeless. I gave him a dollar. Ganneville gave me a magazine. Phénix handed me a flyer for an Indian music concert at Le Grand Café on St-Denis street.

On the Metro platform were two college students, a blond woman and a swarthy man. They clung to each other in an embrace which even the arrival of the train could not break. No one heard what language they were speaking. Everyone knew what language they spoke.

Slow, slow, quick, quick, quick, hold.

AUTUMN

Look up autumn in a thesaurus and you'll find several synonyms. Tender isn't one of them. Yet that's what autumn is. It is the thin skin between warmth and cold, between the youthful cub and the toothless carcass of old age.

Autumn is not a time for beginnings. It is the Jewish New Year but that doesn't make sense here. Maybe there was never an autumn in biblical times. It was just one harvest festival after another. In Asia, Buddhists are celebrating the end of the monsoons and the planting of rice.

We, in the west, are growing nothing. We tidy up our lives, put things in their proper places, and prepare for the cruelest months. There is a last minute burst of activity on the street. Electric saws moan. Renovations have to be finished before the first serious frost hits. Outdoor water lines are drained. Grape arbors are cut back. The last of the tomatoes are pulled from the vines. Late season raspberries are eaten off the cane.

It is autumn. This is the time of year when I am allowed to actually do something. Over the years my repertoire of household skills has been severely curtailed as one minor disaster followed another.

Here is what I am no longer allowed to do: install bookshelves, build anything, weed the garden. In other words, any act of creation or cultivation has been deemed beyond my ken.

Here is what I am allowed to do: tear down walls, remove hazardous waste, compost. In other words, I am Siva the destroyer. It is autumn and my season has come.

Through three seasons, the compost heap has grown within a large black plastic container in a far corner of the garden. We have fed it daily with grass cuttings, coffee grounds, vegetable pairings, mouldy fruit from the back of the refrigerator, and the occasional desiccated plant.

In autumn the pile reaches its zenith. Removing one of the container's side panels reveales a universe. The bottom third of the compost is dark and loamy. It is rich with long worms, the width and colour of my finger. Centipedes, millipedes, and beetles burrow into the earth.

The middle third is a brown wet mulch whose smell has a slightly, sulphorous edge. Thumb size slugs cling to the side.

The top third is barely digested. There are egg shells from a recent omelet and a raft of tomato skins from last weekend's canning. Fruit flies swarm when I lift the top. A squirrel was in there the other day, gnawing a peach pit.

This is my world now. When I was a kid I liked to play in the mud. Now it's my job. I take a pitchfork and pull the humus from the bottom. With each haul, the compost settles further into the container. Soon the middle layer of muck is at the bottom and there is room for a new layer on the top.

I take my treasure and sift it into a neat pile. Twigs, rocks and lumps of clay get tossed to the side. Slowly, the wheelbarrow fills with loam. It is as black as the night, studded with tiny stars of white perlite. I can push my arm up to the elbow and the resistance stays the same. It is firm but giving. The odour is pleasant. It smells of copper and iron, of blood, maybe of life itself.

Soon I will spread this rich earth over a lifeless, leafless garden. Siva's power is awesome. The destroyer is also the restorer. One day, the weather will turn warm again and this thin black blanket will nurture the promise of spring.

—◥—

Here's a great dish for fall that cleans out the kitchen. The ingredients are simple but delicious: left over cookies, dried out cake, and way too many apples.

Thus we have apple cookie crumb pie.

Apple Cookie Crumb Pie

Take 6 cups of left over cookies, stale spice cake and anything else that's dry, sweet and tastes good. Crumb it up in a food processor with three tablespoons of butter or shortening. Add a few drops of water if it doesn't hold together when you ball a little in your hand.

Take an eight inch pie plate and pat a layer of the cookie crumb dough onto the bottom and sides. Put it in a hot (450° F) oven for 10 minutes as you prepare the rest.

Squeeze the juice from one half a lemon into a litre or so of cold water.

Peel, core and thickly slice a half dozen medium-sized apples. You get 8 slices to the apple. Let the slices sit in the lemon water until you're ready to use them. This keeps them from turning brown.

Take the pie shell from the oven. Drain the apples. Mix them with half a dozen tablespoons of blond or brown sugar, a couple of tablespoons of cold butter cut into small chunks, the juice from the other half of the lemon, and a heaping tablespoon of cornstarch.

Mound the apple mixture in the pie shell. Cover with the remaining cookie crumbs. Cook at 350°F for 30 minutes and then at 325°F for another 15 minutes or until the apples are soft.

Serve with heavy cream or ice cream.

SISTER MARY POWER

It was St. Patrick's day, but it was also a Sunday afternoon. So, while much of Montreal enjoyed the parade, Sister Mary Power, of the Society of the Sacred Heart, walked a half hour to a squat brick building in a shabby part of town.

The building on St-Jacques is angled away from the traffic. The cars drive quickly on this stretch of road. Most people wouldn't notice this building, or the half-dozen surveillance cameras around it, or the bars over the windows, or the metal grills behind the bars, or the discrete sign near the bulletproof windows.

The sign says Immigration Prevention Centre, as if wanting to be a Canadian was a disease.

If you're between countries and our federal government doesn't trust you, this becomes your home. If you claim to be a refugee and immigration officials fear you'll disappear, this is where you're sent.

We'd like to believe that everyone who is put behind these bars is a danger to society; that each is here for a good reason. We'd like to believe that people are kept here for only as long as it takes to send them back home.

We don't like to believe that there are women and young children in small rooms, or that they have only a walled-in asphalt court in which to exercise. We don't like to believe that there are people living here for nine and ten months. We don't like to believe that someone could be forced to remain here only because he couldn't find another place to stay.

Some of the people here are criminals, but others lost their way and ended up here. Fortunately, for them and for us, there is Sister Mary Power.

Sister Mary Power is 75. She walks to the Centre every Sunday afternoon and checks on who is there. Occasionally she brings a gift, some cigarettes or a pair of slippers, something to make their lives easier. Mostly she listens to their stories.

The Turk's story. He arrived in Canada with his wife and children. They claimed to be refugees. He and his wife separated before their cases were heard. She went to Toronto and was accepted as a refugee. He stayed in Montreal and his case was rejected. He was put into the Centre. Sister Mary Power found out that his wife had been accepted and helped him appeal. The wife came to the hearing. He was accepted and the family has been together since. "If I hadn't been around he would have been deported," says Sister Mary Power.

"What am I doing? I suppose I'm trying to help them get out," she says. "I've been able to help some who should not have been there. Many people don't know their rights. (The government's) attitude is that they are a security risk. I was even told I could be a hostage. But very few are criminals. Many are poor people. They are going nuts because they aren't able to work and send money to their families."

On Sunday, she visits for a couple of hours. She passes through the bullet-proofed glass doors and climbs a flight of stairs to the cafeteria.

Without the right paper, I can't get in. There is

no immigration official on duty, only uniformed Pinkerton security guards.

Instead of entering, I wait outside. I count the security cameras. I walk around the Econoline and GMC vans that ferry the detainees in caged compartments through the city. A few middle-aged men smile wearily from their rooms. From the second floor, a hand pokes through a small opening in a metal grill and waves.

"Every refugee needs a guardian angel," says Sister Mary Power. Every Sunday afternoon, the detainees meet theirs.

TAI CHI MAN

The water from the fountain flows across granite. The breeze blows silently. An old man jumps.

He takes three hops, this old man in a grey cap and faded trench coat. He is here every morning at 10, a little later than others, more regularly than some. He moves into the tiger and a hand claws the air briefly to signal danger, then into the crane position. His moves are studied and graceful. He is 78 years old and this combination of tai chi and chinese karate come as naturally to his body as breathing.

He makes a large circle of detailed moves in the space between the Palais des Congrès and Complex Guy Favreau. He is dancing through the streets of what once was an extended Chinatown. He is crouching in front of houses that were torn down so that the Federal government could have a set of buildings as large as the Quebec government's Complex Desjardins across the street. With this kind of competititve planning, most of a community was lost.

The old man dances before the doors of the YMCA. At the same time, inside the weight room of the Y, a man in his forties stands before a rack of iron weights. He is dressed in standard gym clothing, shorts, shoes, a t-shirt. He has a thick belt around his waist with straps that go over his shoulders. Chest muscles bulge between the straps. The belt keeps the guts in. It is supposed to help prevent internal injuries. He leans back against a wall and sets a 10 pound weight on his feet. He stands straight and, with his heel planted firmly, uses his toes to pull the weight up. The calf muscles become larger and more defined as he holds the pose. He repeats the movement until he is breathing a little harder. One exercise done.

Around him are separate machines for more than a dozen lifts and presses. There is a back extender, thigh abductors, barbells, a machine to strengthen stomach muscles, another for biceps. There are machines for climbing steps, others for rowing, for cycling, for running endlessly without ever leaving your space. It is a tight enclosed area. The smell of sweat mixes with acrid paint thinner as someone paints a large piece of equipment.

Outside it is spring. The air is sweet after several recent days of rain. For the first time in a week, there is sun. It is warm enough to walk with a light jacket. The old man moves into the familiar form of a tai chi pose. He pushes his hands out from his body, pushing away imaginary walls or enemies, pushing away the ghosts of time.

He keeps moving and does not perspire. He is still wearing his trench coat and cap. His circle becomes smaller. He brings his arm down as sharply as a falling sword. He turns and hops again. He bows deeply at the end.

The old man walks quickly out of the sunlight. He moves into the shadows of the Complex. A moment later he is just another old Chinese man on a green metal bench. The old men and women are always here, sitting, chatting, smoking. They are as much a part of Guy Favreau as the raw brick.

The strong man from the YMCA walks out. His

round of exercise is finished for the day. He walks past the green benches, past the old Chinese men and women who sit through the morning.

A middle-aged Chinese woman now stands in a corner of the square outside. She is moving her arms in a series of exercises. They are not quite calisthenics, not quite martial art. The strong man from the Y walks past her. He walks past her shadow. It cuts through the air as silent as sun.

CHRISTMAS WITH JOSEPH AND MARY

We are in a church. Joseph is describing his situation. Joseph is an accountant. His wife, Mary, is a nurse. They are looking for shelter, not just for a night, but for the rest of their lives. They came here as refugees from Pakistan.

Joseph and his family are Protestants. Pakistan, which is 97% Muslim, adheres to Islamic law. Joseph says that he was involved in church activities. He visited Christian families in the slums and worked with them. He claims that he was beaten several times because of his religious beliefs and says that his experience isn't unusual for Christians in Pakistan. He says that he was told "you are educated, you work in a large company, you should become Muslim."

One day, about two years ago, he was dragged into an army jail where he was tortured and forced to sign a blank page before he was released. That paper was later filled with statements blaspheming the Prophet Mohammed. Such a crime can be punishable by death in Pakistan.

The police came to his house and he fled. He left the capital, Islamabad, and stayed hidden, with the help of church organizations, in other parts of the country for two months. He made his way to Canada where he claimed status as a refugee. Mary and their three children arrived a year later and also asked to be accepted as refugees.

The Immigration and Refugee Board heard his case and denied his claim. The board members did not believe his story and felt that he could return to Pakistan without fear of persecution. Mary's claim was also denied. They said the problems she had in Pakistan were due less to her religion and more because her husband had left.

Their cases are being appealed, but appeals in such matters are usually only heard when some aspect of the law is in dispute.

Mary and Joseph ask those in the church to write to the Minister of Immigration on their behalf. Joseph ends his talk. He says, "The only thing I can request of you is to pray for me, pray for my family." We pray.

That is the story of Mary and Joseph. Maybe the Minister will judge their situation personally and decide to let them stay in Canada as immigrants. He can accept such cases on compassionate grounds. The law gives him that choice. Maybe he, or his department, will decide that their story is false, that there is no religious persecution in Pakistan, although others, with similar stories have been accepted.

It is hard not to hear their story and feel an immense sadness for our world, their family, and our involvement. For we are involved as well.

Everyone tells the story of Joseph and Mary at Christmas. Nobody makes a case for the inn keepers who turned them away or the one who let them stay, if only for a short while, in the manger. But sometimes the inns are full and there is no room. Sometimes it's hard to believe that Mary is as pregnant as she claims or that Joseph and his family can't find another place for the night. After all, inn keepers have to tend to their own as well. They have to take care of their families too and they can't look after everyone.

Inn keepers know that they must keep their distance, that they have to be objective. They can't get involved with each person who comes through the door. If you let in everyone, then you risk losing control of the inn. At least that is what the other inn keepers say.

No one wants to be taken for an easy mark. If the door is always open, maybe you'll be seen as someone who is easily fooled and overly naive. It's a risk that few inn keepers are willing to take.

And what happens if those already in the inn don't like the couple that's just arrived? "That new family that moved in, why are they so different?"

Besides, you never know if someone you let in won't take advantage of you. They might steal your money or stab you in the back. There are some horrible stories around and inn keepers can't be too careful.

Mary and Joseph have a tough story, but inn keepers hear a lot of tough stories. They know that you have to have a broader perspective. That's why it's helpful to look at the big picture. A good inn keeper tends to his ledger.

After all, numbers are manageable. When your quota is reached the "no vacancy" sign gets turned on for the night. Once you've made your decision, that's it. Pack up the books and go upstairs. Don't turn around. It's a lot harder if you have to meet those still left out in the cold.

A RESTAURANT DIES

The pink and white awning on Sherbrooke St. still looks new. The words on it, "Café Sunny buffet cuisine indienne et canadienne," have always promised more than this small restaurant could deliver; more, in fact, than any restaurant has ever been able to deliver here. The phone number is out of service and the windows, which used to be covered with hand lettered daily specials, now have posters plastered on them for a Flamenco Fiesta, a local jazz concert, and "Scotland's Celtic rock supergroup." Inside, a half dozen tables are draped with cloth but the door is locked and probably won't be opened again for a while.

Last year 618 restaurants opened in the Montreal area. Their owners were confident that they could run one of the most difficult and exhausting businesses around. Everyone has a dream. If you're a decent cook, willing to work for free as long as necessary and don't mind the hours, you might even make the dream come true.

Last year 674 restaurants went bankrupt. Other owners eschewed the legal formality, closed the doors and walked away. Many owners find the work too hard, some lose their families, some just don't want to lose any more money. It's a gambler's game. In this city, most restaurants fail in the first three years.

There are plenty of excuses for those that don't

make it. Montrealers don't eat out in January, the weather is too cold in February, the city tore up the sidewalk in the spring, everybody is out of town during the summer, the staff demanded too much money, there are too many similar restaurants in the area

An established owner learns to be a business-man; but a first-time restauranteur is often an opti-mist and a fool. There is always some money com-ing in so there is always hope. There is no more immediate gratification than owning a restaurant and seeing people smile as they eat the food you've just prepared. There is no worse feeling at the end of the day than watching a buffet selection turn cold and greasy with so much food still untouched.

Even a successful restaurant can be an illusion. Suppliers may stake you for a while, the landlord might give you a little leeway in paying the rent. No one wants to see a restaurant fail. It's easy to lose a few thousand a month without ever realizing what is happening, and besides next month might be better. You keep saying that you'll turn the corner until there are no more corners left to turn.

Before its Indian incarnation this was a Caribbean spot and before that a restaurant with French and Spanish regional cooking. It's been a snack bar twice. Lately the real estate agent has been showing the place to an older couple who want to serve Jamaican home cooking.

The owners of Café Sunny tried their best. Ashok Chitra has earned his living as a cook for more than 20 years. He says that before he tried running his own place, he worked in many of Montreal's long-established Indian restaurants including Nataraj and the Bombay Palace. Both he and his wife are good cooks. Ashok was skilled at using the tandoor, the large clay oven common to North Indian cooking. He was a master at the art of making delicate Indian pastries.

Good cooking demands a discerning clientele and Montreal can be a tough town for first-time restaurant owners. Café Sunny had few customers and the specialties were getting made less frequently. Elsewhere, they might have made it; but there were few passersby and parking was difficult. Within a few weeks, Café Sunny had become yet another $5.95 all-you-can-eat Indian buffet. Then there was the competition. The Chitras opened their restaurant in an area with two established places nearby serving similar Indian cooking. By the time Café Sunny closed there were three more Indian restaurants in the neighbourhood.

Ashok and his wife Usha had a dream. They wanted their own business and opened up Café Sunny, named for their three year old son. They opened at the end of the year. It was winter and during a recession; not a good time to start a restaurant in Montreal.

A few weeks ago, Ashok Chitra removed the menus from the windows and took the brightly coloured Indian tapestries off the walls. He said he had lost too much money and that the store had poor insulation and was too cold in the winter. This summer, municipal inspectors said that the electrical wiring should be changed and that might cost $10,000. Ashok cleaned out the tandoor oven and closed the front door for a final time. His words at the end were the same as when he had begun. "You have to take a chance once in a while," he said.

STARDUST

Third floor, Ross Pavilion, Royal Victoria Hospital. The voices are soft. The autumn light is diffused. Even the intercom beseeching "Dr. X., please come to the phone" seems muted. This is the palliative care unit of the Royal Vic.

Twelve men and women are dying. Most have an advanced form of cancer. They are not waiting for emergency measures. Palliate means to ease without curing.

Rather than a ward for dying, here is a place to learn about death. Some patients even return home, better able to control their nausea or other aspects of their illnesses. Many can finally talk about what they are going through with their families.

The staff is caring; but what sets this floor apart is the music. Deborah Salmon is a trained musician and a music therapist. She uses music to help patients and their families relax, deal with pain, tiredness, fear, and depression. A cassette player, donated by Sony, is beside each bed. The floor maintains a library of hundreds of tapes.

On a Friday, Deborah makes her rounds with Monique Bailly, a nurse and accomplished amateur pianist. Monique is training at the palliative care unit while completing a degree in music therapy at UQAM.

The first patient we visit is M., a widower. He

sits in a chair, clutching his stomach and prefers speaking Italian which neither Deborah or Monique know. In any language he communicates that the pain is strong today. Deborah and Monique trundle a cart into the room. It is loaded with a flute, several percussion instruments and a dozen music books with songs and melodies to match every taste. Some of the titles are "Italian Songs, " "Flute Solos," "Universal Show Stoppers," and "Popular Songs that Will Live For Ever."

Deborah hands me a guitar. I strum a few chords. She picks up her flute and softly plays Arrivederci Roma. She asks M. to tell the pain arrivederci. He seems to appreciate the image. His hands move away from his stomach, he relaxes and eventually smiles.

"I assess people," she says later. "I try to see what their relationship is with music and how receptive they are. Music can stimulate emotions. It can be a therapeutic tool for meditation to bring out memories and support morale. It helps people connect with what has been meaningful in their lives."

Mrs. G. is in another room. She used to be a volunteer on this floor. She has not responded since Wednesday night. Her husband watches over her, caressing her with a kiss on the cheek and then moving quickly away. After asking his permission, Monique wheels in an electric piano. Deborah says that she and Monique played frequently when Mrs. G. was alert. Deborah bends over her and says "We're going to play for you. I hope you'll hear us."

Monique improvises something languid, like a Chopin nocturne synchronized to Mrs. G.'s breathing. Deborah slips into the notes with a simple chant. This goes on for a while and Mr. G. seems uncomfortable as if the wake has started and the patient is not quite dead. He has been constantly caring for his wife and the therapists realize that he also needs to be comforted.

Deborah encourages him to choose a song. He picks one of profound sadness, Hoagy Carmichael's Stardust.

"Sometimes I wonder why I spend the lonely night, dreaming of a song. The melody haunts my reverie, and I'm once again with you…"

Across the hall, a jubilant Mme. L. waits for her regular music session. She is 82 and is thin and frail in her pink and white robe. She studied violin half a century ago and pulls the therapists through a repertoire that ranges from "Baby Face" to songs from the Tales of Hoffman. She finishes with Edith Piaf's "Non, je ne regrette rien." "Life without music is boring," says Mme. L. "Don't tell me all of us won't feel better for having had this session."

For the past ten years, Deborah Salmon has walked into these rooms, playing for people who may be gone the following day. I ask her if she has ever played as someone died. She tells me it happens, most recently a few days ago. "When it's working well, I sometimes feel that the patient is letting go." She thinks for a few moments and says "It's a privilege to be with people at that time. There is an essential quality of living in the dying time of their lives."

Before I leave I open the song book again, to Mr. G's choice, Stardust. "… when our love was new and each kiss an inspiration. But that was long ago. Now my consolation is in the stardust of a song."

BLICK

The members of Blick want to talk about two things: another exhibition and how they can help create stability in Montreal.

At least, that's what I think they want. The members of Blick are Russian, at least they speak Russian but none of them admits to being Russian.

"I'm half Finnish" says Tatiana Partanen who does colourful work with acrylics and hubcaps.

"I'm Armenian," says Ekaterina Tarzian, who has participated in a dozen shows since 1980 when she was chosen for Riga's Exposition of Young Painters, "but my home was in Siberia."

"I'm really Bulgarian" says Boyan Markovsky who claims to speak almost every language in eastern Europe, "I am an immigration consultant, also an artists' consultant, also a translator. Here is my card."

"Blick is Russian for flash or reflection," says Markovsky. "No, it means ..." starts Partanen whose English flows into a Russian sea of images of which the only word I can recognize that regularly bobs to the surface is Blick.

Partanen hands me a translation of one of her poems. It is called Dedicated to Kandinsky. "I know everything: movement and colour / Then the triangle cries / From the point."

Blick's meeting room is in Partanen and Tarzian's Stanley street apartment. Paintings cover the walls and are stacked three deep in the corridor. Moscow television journalist, and recent Canadian immigrant, Sergei Moskovitch is there too. He says that he loves Montreal "It is like an ancient city, everything is... octagonal."

Tarzian also says she loves the city "I have status. I have money. Nothing. Emotionally, Montreal is very good for artists. Financially, it is very difficult."

The ashtray fills with cigarettes. Tarzian pours cups of strong, coarsely ground coffee. The air is heavy with Russian. The words come down to me in thick translated bundles.

"... recreate the silver period, from 1900 to 1925, when science, literature, art and theater came together ... multimedia meditative show to induce contemplation to accommodate contemporary people to their surroundings ... an integrative force which is not material..."

"We have had two exhibitions," says Markovsky, showing me copies of the computer art he does. "We had one in Guy Favreau and we are planning another in an Armenian church."

Markovsky has been here for a while. The others arrived in the last year or so. "We feel there is a field here to compensate the bad forces in the universe," says Partanen. " We are creating stability."

Partanen has yet to sell her work in Montreal but she says that she is positive. The others agree. They are all positive. They know that people who have lived their lives here mope, that living in Montreal is depressing. Moskovitch smiles and says "you don't know what real famine is."

Moskovitch says he has leads for a television series. Markovsky shows me an idea he has for the Canadian government to use some of Blick's paintings as postage stamps. Tarzian is working on icons for the Armenian church show.

A rough version of Bruegel's Tower of Babel is on an easel at the front of the room. The 16th century painting shows that people can't work together once they stop communicating. "For us, it is a symbol of our times," says Markovsky.

Markovsky's wife comes to take him home. She has been working for an investment company for a year. "Investing is good," she says, "what do you do?" I say I'm a writer. "Oh," she says and the pitch stops. "Boyan," she says to Markovsky, "I have to go to day care. You can stay but be home by 6, 6:15 at the latest.

"Artists," she says looking at me. "They are not like normal people. They can work 25 hours a day and I won't get any sleep."

KHELA'S TRUCK DRIVING SCHOOL

It's an entrepreneur's office, small, functional and sparse. There's a phone, a fax machine, and a coffee maker. A cell phone lies folded on a desk taking up a third of the room. Half-a-dozen chairs are pushed against one wall.

There are a few regulatory permits and certificates, neatly framed. One is for graduating from a skid control school.

A laminated picture of a 60 foot Kenworth truck hangs behind the desk. The picture is plugged into the wall. The cab and semitrailer are in perfect focus. Clearance and marker lights glow where real lights would be. The picture is called "King of the Road" and it has a few extra details.

On the side of the trailer are the words "peace & liberty." A Punjabi phrase for "the grace of God" floats in the sky above the rig. The Kenworth's grille sports the Nishan Sahib, the Sikh emblem with the double-edged sword symbolizing truth and justice.

In the next room, an instructor was giving eight men and women a lesson in driving theory. The course was in Bengali. Others practiced written exams on computers. Occasionally the phone rang as people called about the $28 "Asian ride carpool service" to Toronto.

Santokh Singh Khela sat at the desk and oversaw everything. Several Sikh men and a couple of Latin Americans stood near him, waiting for truck driving lessons.

José Madrid Gomez was one of them. He's 53 and works for Moisson Montreal. He likes his job but he wanted to build some security by getting a truck driver's license. He also wanted to show his four sons "that you're never too old to improve yourself."

Look at your driver's license. Like mine, you probably have a class 5 permit. That lets us drive a car. Maybe you have a class 4, good for taxis, emergency vehicles and small buses. Those driving small trucks need a class 3. MUCTC bus drivers need a class 2.

But if you want the romance of being "King of the Road," of travelling across the country in a rig with a 53 foot van, of earning perhaps $70,000 a year, for that you need a class 1.

Khela has a class 1. He got his permit in 1985 when there were maybe three or four Sikh truck drivers in Montreal. He figured there might be 2000 now. He thought 400 of them might even have their own trucks.

Every era seems to get an immigrant group ready to do the jobs no one else wants. Once, in this town, Jews sweated in the garment industry. Once Italian men were stone masons, the Chinese did the laundry, the Ukrainians had a monopoly on window washing, Black women were maids, the Greeks ran the restaurants, and every live-in-nanny was Filipino. These days it may be Sikhs and transportation.

After I met Khela, I called up the Canadian Trucking Human Resources Council. The Council's Lynda Harvey told me that Canada faces a shortage of truck drivers, perhaps 20,000 in the next few years. Harvey said "it's the job with the highest average age, few youth are coming in." I asked her if she had noticed a lot of Sikhs in the business. "Come to think of it," she said, "I was at a trade show in Calgary and there were a lot of Sikhs. I wonder why that's so."

"It's a good business for us," Khela said. He looked at a picture on the wall, the Golden Temple in Amritsar. "Even there, in India, Sikhs are involved in transportation. We value independence," he continued. "We don't like to work for other people. Driving, you are free."

ARTEM THE KNIFE SELLER

Artem the knife seller, showed up the other day. He was trying out a new line. "These are kitchen tools that are guaranteed for life with handles that won't melt on the fridge." I said that he probably meant the stove. He looked puzzled. I explained that a fridge was that big thing in the kitchen that keeps the food cold and a stove was for cooking.

Artem needs to improve his English; but that's one of the reasons he wanted this job. Two years ago he was at our border, three days out of Russia. He was 15 and had come with his mother and an older cousin. They were refugees from Kazakhstan.

After Russia, Kazakhstan is the largest country in what was once the USSR. Independence came in 1991. Since then, Russians, who are usually Christian, aren't as much appreciated by the larger, predominantly Muslim, Kazahk population.

Tatiana, Artem's mother, said the family was fleeing discrimination and persecution. They followed the standard procedure and formally applied to our government to be accepted as refugees. Two years later, they are still waiting to hear whether they can stay.

During that time, the family moved into my neighbourhood. Slowly, they entered our culture. Artem, picked up English from his neighbours and learned French at Saint-Luc, a local high school with a strong immersion program. He helped a community group set up its computers. He found a girlfriend.

Now he was at our dining room table. It was demonstration time. He pulled out a cutting board from a large, soft-sided sales case. He laid out a wad of leather, picked up a small serrated knife and sliced through the material. He took a length of rope and showed me how easily another of his knives could cut through it. I tried the same trick with a knife from our kitchen. It bounced off the leather.

Two years ago Artem was just another refugee. Now he was honing his pitch, with occasional glances at handwritten notes, to make sure he remembered to tell me every detail.

He pulled out the "fisherman's special," a knife with a long, impressively sharp blade and a detachable handle. He took a penny and, with his company's special scissors, cut the coin into a long copper curl.

I listened to his spiel and a memory flashed by. It was a few days after he was in Canada. Tatiana was bargaining for a television set at a Salvation Army store. She wanted a TV in the home to help her son learn a new language. So on day 1, Artem arrived in Canada. On day 2 the family found an apartment in NDG. On day 3, he was watching Newswatch. Now it was day 752.

As Artem packed up his sales kit, I asked him about his plans. He said that he had enrolled at Dawson for the fall to study commerce. In two years, the shy kid from Kazakhstan has become a Canadian. Now all he has to do is find out if he can stay.

THE GRINCH THAT STOLE SPRING

It has been a long cold winter on the street. When we go to sleep, it's April. When we wake, it feels like November again. It is almost a month past the equinox and we are desperate for a sign of Spring. Last week, we thought we had one.

If you had walked down our street on one of those few tantalizingly warmer days, you might have seen a huge old maple towering above the houses, half a block down. A few spigots were tapped into the trunk. They were stuck into holes the size of a quarter.

Thin hoses snaked from the spigots and dipped into five gallon bottles. You could stand on the sidewalk, reach up and touch a spigot. The sap that dripped into the hoses was thin and clear and slightly sweet. If you had never tasted maple syrup you wouldn't have known what it was; however we knew. It was our promise of spring, drops of liquid gold.

The maple was in Pierre and Lisa's yard. Pierre is from Quebec but his wife is from California. This was an incomparable gift to end our brutal winter, home made maple syrup. It takes about 40 liters of sap to make one of syrup. That's about how much Pierre ended up with last year. We were given a small bottle. The syrup was dark, pungent, woody and rich. It went well with pancakes.

This year Pierre set up his tap lines again. Here

was someone on the street, only a few kilometers from downtown Montreal, making maple syrup. We watched the sap slowly work its way into the bottles. A few days later they were gone. At first we thought someone had stolen the sap. Then we thought it might have been because of the bottles. They were the size of demijohns. They're used for filtered water dispensers and sell for about $5 each. The next day snow fell again.

Pierre got a notice from the city a couple of days later. On our street, the City of Montreal owns the land from the sidewalk to a few feet before the houses. The gardens, the trees, the ornate brickwork we've layed down all technically belong to the city.

Pierre's tree , it turns out, is on public land. It doesn't matter that when it's leaves fall, Pierre is the one who rakes them up. It doesn't matter that Pierre is the one who mows the grass in the small yard behind the tree, or that he built a fence in front and keeps it neat and painted white. All of this, it turned out, was the city's. Making maple syrup from the tree contravened regulation number 7935, article 4 and a dutiful municipal employee is coming to see him soon.

So Pierre waits for an inspector from the division of horticulture and park maintenance to pay him a visit. He wonders who reported him for tapping his own tree and who stole the large jars that were filling with sap. We watch the snow fall on our street. We wonder who is the grinch who stole Spring.

BILL'S BENCH

The other day Bill brought over a bench. It's an ordinary bench in every way except that you couldn't buy it anywhere. We tried the bench at the nearest Canadian Tire. There was one in front of the store near the center of the mall. It had a lot of wood and wrought iron and a dip towards the back that invited slouching. It didn't feel too comfortable after a few minutes.

Bill's bench doesn't invite slouching. It's three hand hewn pieces of two inch thick pine. Thick dowels are angled underneath the seat to keep it true. The bench is no nonsense and solid. If it rocks a bit, the problem is with the floor.

I sit down on Bills' bench and automatically sit up straight. My chest pushes out a little. My stomach is a little flatter. It's not a bench. It's the Marines.

We asked Bill to build us a bench because we knew we wouldn't be able to find something this simple, this good. We had to replace an old bench that worked well for a dozen or so years until the plywood started splintering. Bill's bench is as solid as a Sunday sermon.

It is what it is: a bench. It's too small to use as a coffee table. You can't put two together and end up with a hide-a-bed.

The seat is long enough to comfortably seat two adults or three kids. It's almost a foot wide. It supports me through the thighs and stays stable even if I pick up my legs and rock them back and forth. It's just the right height so that, as I sit, I'm balanced on the balls of my feet. I'm relaxed but kept alert, ready to jump up should I need to protect the fortress behind me.

A house needs a good bench. The porch or balcony are the entry ways to the home, not quite public, not quite private. Once a sentry would stay out here. Today it's the bench.

Benches create companionship the way a chair can never hope to. You can't pat a chair the way you can a bench and invite someone to sit right next to you, maybe even a little closer than normal social custom would allow.

In public places, benches get shunted into the parks, not the really interesting commercial spaces. Those are given to outdoor tables and chairs. "Sit here," the chairs seem to say, "buy a café-au-lait, order the seafood salad croissant. You want to stay here and do nothing? Beat it! Go and find a bench."

Benches get coffee in Styrofoam cups and maybe a bag of Munchkins. They get strangers who might have something in common.

With chairs and a table, people have to look at each other. This can be irksome, even boring after a while. Benches make you look out. Talk yields to contemplation.

Bill's bench is of it's type, and perfect. Right now it is simple, unfinished pine. Soon, we will put a couple of coats of paint on it and move it outside. I'm not ready for that. It sits in the office. It gets moved to the living room or does extra duty at the dinner table. It gets admired for its simple aesthetics, for its finely sanded surface and perfectly rounded corners.

Not too long ago, a bench was something people made for themselves and took for granted. As intelligent or clever as I like to think I am, Bill's bench reminds me of what I'm incapable of doing, such as constructing something simple, like a bench.

SWIMMING

It is a perfect summer evening and the Montreal West pool is filled with a surge of green suits and white foam. It is warm up time. Kids from less than eight years of age to over 18 are doing laps. They swim in their lanes, the water rising between them. The youngest ones pause every few meters to walk a couple of steps, the older ones move rhythmically, doing powerful breast strokes or elegant butterflies. Their bodies arc, their arms barely bruising the water with strong, confident strokes.

It hurts to watch such beauty. We, the parents, will never again move as smoothly or breath as effortlessly. We'll never feel quite the grace of motion that these young athletes possess.

The teams come out of the water and retreat to opposite sides of the pool. The coaches gather their squads around. They yell cheers to lift their spirits. They hurl out curses to terrorize their foes. The kids scream and the energy is fearsome, but the cheers themselves are unlikely to cause much damage.

One goes:
We've got spirit – Yes we do.
We've got spirit– How about you?
Another is a fribble:
Give me a B – Give me a B
Give me another B – Give me another B
Give me one last B – What does that spell?

(Flap right index finger over lips while making a buh-buh-buh sound and point the other index finger at the opposing team).

The swimmers line up at the end of the pool and the competition goes through a comfortable repetitive pattern. The meet moves progressively through the age groups and strokes: free style, back stroke, breast, fly and then relay races. We parents exhort our kids on, congratulate the winners, and commiserate with the rest.

Few people pull out cellular phones during the meet. Maybe they turn them off for a few warmly isolating hours.

We concentrate on the form and the effort. There aren't too many decisions to make. Red licorice laces are two for a quarter, coffee is 75 cents, a raffle ticket costs a buck. The proceeds go to help the team.

Everyone competes. Almost everyone who finishes wins something. First place in each race gets a red ribbon. Second is blue, fifth is purple, sixth is green. Summer is golden.

There is another world that exists outside this small slice of perfection; but it is not the world of endless swimming with a train horn sounding in the distance and the sun slowly dipping through red on the horizon. The world outside this pool is both fearful and fearsome. The news is of calamities, of floods in Europe and terrorist bombings; but on this sweet evening, a hundred or so kids and their parents are secluded. They are here to swim, on a warm summer night.

MR. MAYO RETIRES

As far as I know, nobody's giving Carlos Mayo a gold watch when he retires. Nobody from the executive suite will shake his hand and give him a little something extra when he locks the door at Rosedale Valet and Tailors for the last time. Nobody's planning a party to thank him for opening at 7 a.m. and shutting around 6 p.m., often later, six days a week, so that everyone on the street can get their cleaning and mending done when its convenient for them, not for him.

There's a picture of Mayo Sr. on the back wall at Rosedale. It's a black and white photo, taken around 1947. There's a lean man with a hint of a smile, maybe in his 40s. He's leaning forward, wearing a t-shirt. You can't help but notice the biceps. They're rock solid from years of shoveling coal on freighters. There's no old picture of Mayo Sr. He died shortly after this one was taken. He was on a trip to Africa, got malaria and died. A month after Mayo Sr. was buried, his son left school to support the family. Carlos Mayo was 14 and began to learn the tailor's trade.

Mr. Mayo has been at Rosedale for nine years. He worked most of his life at a big company, International Ski and Leisure. He pressed, he sewed, he cut, he learned the trade. He designed the motorcycle jackets and pants cops used to have when they rode the beat with sidecars.

Hanging among the dry cleaning at Rosedale is a pair of wool pants. They look like formal riding breeches. The elderly gentleman who ordered them no longer drives a motorcycle but he gets the legs cut narrow along the lower inseam so the pants will fit comfortably into the boots he still likes to wear.

There are three old Singer sewing machines and a wooden replica of large tailor's shears in one window. A couple of red wool jackets with white leather sleeves hang in the other, waiting for the right high school or college football team to come along. Mr. Mayo still makes them to order.

For most of the years, there were two tailors at Rosedale. Then, as business slowed, it was down to one. Soon Mr. Mayo will lay down the shears. Soon it will be time to stop getting up at 5 a.m. for his long commute into Montreal. Soon it will be time to enjoy the grandchildren who live on the other side of town. Gold watch or not, it's time to go.

Looking for a business in a prime west end location? Mr. Mayo won't sell Rosedale to just anyone. "If all they want is dry cleaning, I'm not interested," he says. "I want to find someone who knows how to be a tailor. These days, someone goes into the needle trade, he learns to be a presser, or he sews parts of jackets. No one today learns the whole trade."

The street doesn't need another dry-cleaner. There are two just down the block. What it needs is a trade. Come July 1, Mr. Mayo takes his with him.

NIGHT RIDER

Gerard Senecal rides the night. "I like to go out after work," he says. "It's quiet, I'm alone, and the city is beautiful." Gerard is over forty and he rides an old but serviceable ten speed. It's late at night, when most of us are either lining up at the clubs or dropping off to sleep; but here, on the Lachine canal, he is one of many late night cyclists moving in silence like the whispers of a ghost. We pass another ghost, a young woman in a long white T-shirt roller-blading alone. Soon we are the only ones on the path. Gerard glances back. "I ride here at least once a week," he says "but the adrenalin still pumps when I crest a hill slowly or come out of a tunnel into the dark. In some ways this could be a dangerous place."

Dangerous perhaps, but there is a beauty which keeps bringing him back. I have ridden the Lachine canal many times but never at this hour. At night the city is transformed. For several years, the back cover of our Yellow Pages used to quote Ed Sullivan of all people. He had mentioned in his New York City newspaper column that he had flown over Montreal and seen a "city of light." Tonight, a warm Thursday night with a clear sky and no wind, the city has a blue, gold, green and red iridescence. If there could be a rainbow at night, it would be electric and it would be the face of Montreal shimmering in the harbour.

"People don't appreciate what we have," says Gerard. "The old port has been cleaned up, the locks were refitted. A tremendous amount of work was done to make this not only historically accurate but enjoyable."

The clock tower was built as a WWI memorial. It was abandoned for years but tonight it is rimmed with spotlights and shines like a platinum ingot. Across the harbour inlet, Bonescours market is bathed in light and mirrored in the water. Foot and cycling bridges are outlined with strips of white Christmas lights and a fountain falls in sheets of electric blue into a reflecting pool. If Disneyland's creators had tried their hand on a small version of Venice, it would be the Old Port at night.

"I love moving outside at night," says Gerard. "In the winter I ski on the mountain. Once I got used to the trails, knew where the ruts and the turns were, I could go almost as fast as during the day. I used to like to kayak in Lake St-Louis at night but there are too many cigarette boats out now. Like those on Miami Vice. I don't know where so many people get the money to own them. I heard it costs a thousand dollars just for a weekend's worth of fuel."

Now, we are above the city, as close to flight as it may be possible on a bicycle, slowly climbing higher on the walkway of the Jacques Cartier bridge. To the right is la Ronde with music and excitement and a neoned Ferris wheel whose glyph hints of the summer of '67. To the left the city lies fat and glowing under countless amber street lamps. Beneath us the coast guard's catamaran – FCG Smith – cuts upstream toward her berth opposite Habitat. We stop and can just hear the wake as the boat passes beneath. "Ahoy," yells Gerard and a figure near the bow looks up and waves. This could never happen during the day, two cyclists and a boat make contact with a hundred and fifty feet of air between them. All at once, Montreal is a quiet small town.

We coast onto île Ste-Hélène, leave la Ronde behind and head deeper into the island's blackness. This is a forest and country road. Gerard's feeble headlight is strong enough to be seen but too weak to do more than pierce the night. I am a hundred yards ahead with only the stars and the lights of a distant Montreal. I'm cycling almost blind, listening to the quiet whirr of the wheels and exhilarated by being alone and my speed which seems faster in the dark. The softest of touches startles me. My ankle is brushed by the wing of a sea gull, crippled and struggling on the road.

We cross the island and circle around, seeing our first car as we climb onto the Concorde bridge. The cars come in bunches with clusters of busses between them, all heading to or from the casino. It is only midnight, but with the noise, traffic and sudden brightness, we are heading into a manic midnight rush hour. "I love this city," Gerard says; but he turns his bike away from the road and the noise and keeps to the canal. Even close relationships occasionally require distance.

<hr />

Cities are organic. Any city that has a soul will show at night. That's if you feel comfortable wandering without a real destination, after midnight. If you can do that, you're in a city worth living in. Montreal lets you do that and that's why we love her.

After midnight, there are few things that draw the

evening out better than that last glass of wine; but when the weather turns chilly we want something comforting. Late at night, its cocoa.

For each cup:
2 marshmallows
1 tablespoon unsweetened cocoa powder,
   such as Fry's
1/2 tablespoon sugar
1 tablespoon milk
1 cup milk

Using a blender, mix the sugar, cocoa and 1 tablespoon of milk together until it is a uniformly dense paste without any lumps. Heat the cup of milk and add it to the cocoa paste. Add one marshmallow and blend until it is frothy.

Serve hot with the other marshmallow on top. Ahh, go ahead... throw in a shot of Kaluha. Enjoy.

PRINTED AND BOUND
IN BOUCHERVILLE, QUÉBEC, CANADA
BY MARC VEILLEUX IMPRIMEUR INC.
IN NOVEMBER, 1997